QUICK NORDIC KNITS

50 Socks, Hats and Mittens

ANN-MARI NILSSON

Trafalgar Square
North Pomfret, Vermont

First published in the United States of America in 2010 by
Trafalgar Square Books, North Pomfret, Vermont 05053

Originally published in Sweden in 2009 by
Hemslöjdens förlag (Handcraft Publishers)
Swedish Handcraft Association: www.hemslojdensforlag.se
ISBN 978-1- 57076-469-1
Library of Congress Control Number: 2010932943

This book has been printed with contributions from, among others, the
Längmanska Cultural Foundation and the Barbro Osher Pro Suecia
Foundation.

ENGLISH TRANSLATION: Carol Huebscher Rhoades
COVER PHOTO: Spruce sock, Baggy hat, Stocking mitten, and Beret.
DESIGNS AND INSTRUCTIONS: Ann-Mari Nilsson
TEXT: Ann-Mari Nilsson, Kerstin Paradis Gustafsson
PHOTOS: Nisse Peterson, Anders Qwarnström (pages 82-84)
ILLUSTRATIONS: Ann-Mari Nilsson
GRAPHIC DESIGN: Eva Kvarnström
EDITOR: Sophia Lundquist
TECHNICAL EDITING: Karin Kahnlund
REFERENCE GROUP: Andersson Åhlin, Ulrika Svensson, Anna Åhlin
PUBLISHER EDITOR: Jan Pilerö, BokåTryck (Bokå Printing)
PRINTING: Fälth & Hässler. Värnamo 2009
SWEDISH PUBLISHER'S EDITOR: Jan Pilerö, BokåTryck (Bokå Printing)

10 9 8 7 6 5 4 3 2 1
Printed in China

ABOUT THE AUTHOR

Ann-Mari Nilsson trained at Beckman's and has extensive textile experience, primarily as a designer for industry. She has designed for Marc
O'Polo, IKEA, Östergötland's Wool Mill and handcraft organizations.
Quick Nordic Knits is Ann-Mari Nilsson's third book in conjunction
with the Swedish Handcraft Association.

TABLE OF CONTENTS

4 Foreword
5 Read this Section First

HATS

8 Baggy
10 Scraps, Heavy Scraps
12 Spruce
14 Cables
16 Ribbed
18 Stars
20 Flaps
22 The Other Direction
24 Bonnet, Heavy Bonnet
26 Stocking Cap
28 Checked
30 Stripes
32 Beret, Heavy Beret
34 Cuffed Beanie
36 Skull Cap

MITTENS

38 Baggy
40 Scraps, Heavy Scraps
42 Spruce
44 Cables
46 Tweed
48 Flaps
50 Bonnet, Heavy Bonnet
52 Stocking, Heavy Stocking
54 Checked
56 Blocks
58 Wrist Warmers
60 Stars

SOCKS

63 Stars
66 Baggy
68 Spruce
70 Ragg, Heavy Ragg
72 Blocks
74 Tweed
76 Spiral, Heavy Spiral
78 Ankle Warmers

82 Wool – a Fantastic Natural Material

FOREWORD

THIS BOOK has instructions for small knitted items, each marked with the level of knitting experience needed to make it.

It is also a reference book with a variety of designs, methods of knitting, patterns, shaping options, wrist warmers, thumbs, and heels that you can mix and match to make your own garments. You'll also find several color suggestions as inspiration. You don't have to be tied to seasonal styles of fashion and color. You can be trendy and avant garde or you can choose classic and timeless styles.

Whatever you choose, you'll have an environmentally friendly wool garment that you'll value and regard in a totally different way than a purchased garment. You will have created something lasting, often with memories knitted in. Who knows, it might end up being patched and remade, and inspire future generations.

I assume that you already know all the knitting basics and have knitted for a while. If that isn't the case, you should buy a knitting handbook or ask someone to help you learn to knit. A warning is in order here: once you've begun to knit it is difficult to stop. For many knitters, the process is often the goal.

Please promise that you will read the chapter Read this Section First before you begin knitting!

A warm thank you to Östergötland's Wool Mill for donating yarn and the Regional Museum in Kristianstad for inspiration for the Spruce design.

Ann-Mari Nilsson

READ THIS SECTION FIRST

INSTRUCTIONS Quickly read through the instructions before you begin knitting so that you will have an idea of what will happen. As you knit, read ahead because sometimes the instructions for the next step extend over a few sentences.

YARN No particular brand of yarn is recommended for these patterns. Use the wool yarns you already have on hand or can obtain easily. It is important, however, that you match the number of yards/meters in 3.5 ounces / 100 grams. Wool yarn with the number 1 = 1000 meters/kilo = 100 meters per 100 grams. 6/2 (six-two) is a two-ply yarn and each strand is 600 m/100 g. When the single strands are plied, that makes it 300 m /100 g which is between a fingering and sport weight or Craft Yarn Council of America standard sizes 1-2 (super fine to fine). The Östergötland's Wool Mill yarn (Visjö 150 m/50g) was used by the author the website is www.ullspinneriet.com. In the patterns that use doubled yarn, you could substitute 6/4 yarn or 3/2. Don't be afraid to try different yarns.

For help choosing a suitable yarn substitution contact one of the suppliers below or your local yarn shop for help. There are numerous yarn suppliers and useful information that can be found on the internet.

Webs—America's Yarn Store
www.yarn.com
customerservice@yarn.com

Halcyon Yarn
www.halcyonyarn.com
service@halcyonyarn.com

Nordic Fiber Arts
www.nordicfiberarts.com
info@nordicfiberarts.com

Vävstuga Swedish
Weaving and Folk Arts
www.vavstuga.com
office@vavstuga.com

GAUGE One of the most important factors in knitting is the gauge or tension. If your gauge doesn't match the one given in the pattern, then the garment will be too big or too little. Always knit a gauge swatch if you are uncertain. We all have different ways of knitting. Change to smaller or larger needles if necessary.

SIZING All the garments in this book are sized for "adult woman." The average is hat size 22 in / 56 cm, hand width 3-3 ¼ in / 7.5-8 cm, and shoe sizes US 7 ½-8 ½ / UK 5-6 / European 38-39. Even in this regard we are different. Measure and compare with something you already have that fits well and size the new garment based on that. Try on mittens and socks as you knit.

CASTING ON Always cast on with two needles held together and then carefully remove the extra needle.

PATTERNS When you are choosing among the various models and knitting methods, take into consideration that two-color stranded knitting takes more stitches because it pulls in the knitted fabric somewhat. Perhaps the new stitch count doesn't allow the shaping to be spaced evenly, but, for the most part, that doesn't matter. It won't be obvious so knit on.

Also consider that two-color knitting is warmer than plain stockinette because the strands on the back trap insulating air. If there are long sections between color changes in the pattern, you need to twist the yarns around each other on the wrong side at least every 3rd st and sometimes on every other stitch to catch the unused yarn.

Every so often, stretch out the knitting on the right needle so that it doesn't pull in.

DOUBLE-POINTED NEEDLES Tighten the yarn a bit as you move from one double-pointed needle to the next so avoid a loose row up the knitting.

INCREASING Whenever you pick up extra stitches at the thumb, fingers, and heels or increase for a thumb gusset, remember to twist those stitches so that they won't make a hole in the knitting. Sometimes you might pick up more extra stitches than suggested around, for example, the thumb and then decrease them on the next row. One method for increasing is to pick up the strand between two stitches and knit into its back loop to avoid a hole (= m1).

METHODS OF KNITTING Stockinette (stocking stitch) worked back and forth sometimes looks a little uneven because purl stitches are often looser than knit stitches. If that happens, work the purl rows with a size smaller needle.

Many knitters avoid purling except for ribbing and occasional rows. Most of the patterns in this book are worked as stockinette in the round even when the surface looks purled. An excellent way to avoid several purled rows is to turn the work inside out and knit, for example, a rolled edging or welt.

SPLICING YARN If you run out of yarn while knitting, you can splice on the new skein. Feather the ends of the old and new yarns and overlap the strands, moisten the overlap area with saliva, and then roll the yarn quickly between your palms. Moisture, warmth, and friction make the fibers stick to each other for an invisible and strong join between the yarn ends.

SHAPING FINGER TIPS The stitch count on glove fingers does not always work for an even repeat of k2, k2tog as recommended. Work the decrease repeats as well as you can. You'll have a finger tip in any case.

HAT CROWN When you are down to 6-8 sts around, you don't need to use all four double-pointed needles. You can easily divide the sts onto 2 parallel dpn, and knit with a third.

FINISHING When all but the final row of decreases have been made, work the last decrease row and tighten the stitch loops one by one at the same time for a smooth finishing.

BLOCKING When a garment is fresh off the needles and all the ends have been woven in, it might feel a little hard and inflexible. Maybe it rolls in the wrong direction and the sizing isn't perfect. The final step in the knitting process is blocking. Block by dampening the garment in lukewarm water and then centrifuge (spin) it in the machine or roll it in a hand towel and gently squeeze out the water. Don't be afraid to gently pull the knitting into shape. Mittens, socks, and even berets can be laid out flat to dry. Hats can be blocked to just smaller than the head size over a hand towel rolled up inside a plastic bag – using only a towel might stretch out the knitting.

WASHING Don't wash your handknits unnecessarily! Every so often just air them out. If the garment is really dirty, then you should wash it. Wash handknits gently by hand (no wringing) in wool wash and lukewarm water; rinse several times in the same temperature water. Next, follow the steps for Blocking, beginning at "centrifuging."

BRUSHING The sturdier mittens in this book, those knit with doubled or tripled yarn, will be even warmer and softer if you turn them inside out and brush them with a hard brush or handcard.

MENDING Keep an eye on your handknits so you notice when they are starting to wear out because it is easier to mend them before they get holes. Mend with duplicate stitch over the worn stitches and those surrounding them. Use a blunt tapestry needle and follow the path of the stitch row. If you still get holes in the garment, it is easiest to repair the hole by sewing on a bit of *vadmal* (woven felt). You can even rip out the section and re-knit it, particularly thumbs, toes, and simple heels.

THUMBS AND HEELS The various methods have different functions and degrees of difficulty.

The easiest thumb to make is a straight thumb where you knit in a strand of waste yarn at the thumbhole. This makes the mitten the same width all the way up the hand. These mittens still fit well and make it easy to maintain patterning. By increasing for a thumb gusset and knitting in waste yarn at the thumbhole, you will have a mitten that is tighter on the lower hand. If you have narrow hands this will fit well. A side gusset makes a mitten with plenty of room for the lower hand.

A simple heel with a band decrease is made the same way as for the top of a mitten. It is fast and easy to knit but doesn't always fit perfectly as would a sock with a heel flap that has more stitches to fit over the instep. In this book we used three variations of the heel flap. Personally I almost always knit simple thumbs and heels.

The drawing below shows the names of the parts of the heel that are used in this book's instructions.

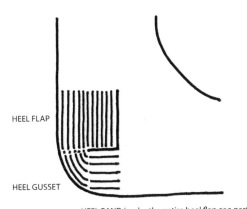

HEEL FLAP

HEEL GUSSET

HEEL BAND (under the entire heel flap or a part of it)

Abbreviations

Beg	begin, beginning
BO	bind off (= British cast off)
cm	centimeter(s)
CO	cast on
dec	decrease
dpn	double-pointed needles
g	gram(s)
in	inch(es)
inc	increase
k	knit
k2tog	knit 2 together
m	meter(s)
m1	make 1 = lift strand between 2 sts and knit into back loop
mm	millimeter(s)
ndl(s)	needle(s)
oz	ounce(s)
p	purl
rem	remain, remaining
rep	repeat
rnd(s)	round(s)
RS	right side
ssk	slip 1 knitwise, slip 1 knitwise, knit together through back loops
st(s)	stitch(es)
tbl	through back loop(s)
WS	wrong side
yo	yarnover (= British yarn forward or yarn around needle)
yds	yard(s)

gauge = British tension
seed stitch = British moss stitch
stockinette = British stocking st

hats
BAGGY

How baggy the hat will be depends on how long you knit before shaping the top: 2 in / 5 cm longer than in the instructions suggest and it really hangs out; 2 in / 5 cm shorter and the hat fits perfectly around the head. The lice pattern makes it warm.

LEVEL OF DIFFICULTY Intermediate

YARN 6/2 wool yarn, 328 yds / 300 m per 100 g

YARN AMOUNTS color 1 red 1.6 oz/45 g, color 2 white .7 oz/20 g

NEEDLES set of 5 dpn US sizes 1.5 and 2.5 / 2.5 and 3 mm

GAUGE 27 sts in pattern on larger needles = 4 in / 10 cm. Adjust needle sizes to obtain correct gauge if necessary.

FINISHED MEASUREMENTS circumference 21 in / 53 cm, length 10 ¼ in / 26 cm

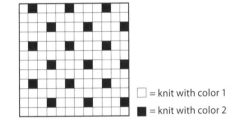

☐ = knit with color 1
■ = knit with color 2

With color 1 and smaller dpn, CO 144 sts. Divide sts evenly over 4 dpn (= 36 sts per dpn) and join, being careful not to twist cast-on row. Work around in k2, p2 ribbing for 5/8 in / 1.5 cm = 6 rnds.

Change to color 2 and continue in ribbing for another 5/8 in / 1.5 cm.

Change to larger dpn, color 1, and lice pattern (see chart). Make sure that color 2 is stranded well on WS so that the knitting doesn't pull in. Work in lice pattern for 6 ¼ in / 16 cm.

TOP SHAPING After completing a single color rnd, k2tog at the beginning and end of each dpn (8 sts decreased on each dec rnd). Dec the same way on every other rnd until 24 sts rem and then dec on every rnd until 8 sts rem. Cut yarn and pull through remaining sts. Weave in ends neatly on WS.

SCRAPS (HEAVY SCRAPS)

Scraps is the easiest hat you can knit with knit stitches throughout. It's even easier when you use doubled yarn.

LEVEL OF DIFFICULTY Easy

YARN SINGLE (DOUBLED) 6/2 wool yarn, 328 yds / 300 m per 100 g

YARN AMOUNTS color 1 red 1 oz/30 g (black 1.4 oz/40 g),
color 2 yellow-green 1 oz/30 g (yellow-green 1.4 oz/40 g)

NEEDLES set of 5 dpn US size 2.5 / 3 mm (US 6 / 4 mm)

GAUGE 26 (19) sts in stockinette = 4 in / 10 cm.
Adjust needle size to obtain correct gauge if necessary.

FINISHED MEASUREMENTS circumference 21 (21 ¾) in / 53 (55) cm,
length 8 in / 20 cm

With color 1, CO 136 sts with single strand or 104 sts
with doubled yarn. Divide sts evenly over 4 dpn and join,
being careful not to twist cast-on row. Work around in
stockinette for 1 ¼ in / 3 cm = 12 (10) rnds. Turn work
inside out so that the purl side faces out = rolled edge.
Change to color 2 and continue in wide stockinette stripes
of 6 (5) rnds each. Catch unused color every 3 (2) rnds.
Knit 8 (7) stripes = about 4 ¾ (4 ¼) in / 12 (11) cm.

You can vary the hat a bit by continuing the reverse stockinette as for the rolled edge (for example, 7 stripes) all the
way up to the top shaping. See Scraps mittens for how to
work the color changes.

TOP SHAPING Dec 8 sts on every other rnd by knitting 2
together at the center and end of each dpn until 8 sts remain. Knit these 8 sts around for 8 (6) rnds. Cut yarn and
pull through rem sts; weave in tails neatly on WS.

SPRUCE

The spruce pattern used for this hat is a fun pattern to play around with. The hat fits the head closely and the seed stitch brim is very soft.

LEVEL OF DIFFICULTY Intermediate

YARN 6/2 wool yarn, 328 yds / 300 m per 100 g

YARN AMOUNTS color 1 gray 1 oz/30 g, color 2 white .7 oz/20 g

NEEDLES set of 5 dpn US sizes 1.5 and 2.5 / 2.5 and 3 mm

GAUGE 27 sts in two-color stranded knitting on larger ndls
= 4 in / 10 cm.
Adjust needle sizes to obtain correct gauge if necessary.

FINISHED MEASUREMENTS circumference 21 in / 53 cm,
length 8 ¼ in / 21 cm

☐ = knit with color 1
■ = knit with color 2

Begin with a slip knot holding colors 1 and 2 together.
With smaller dpn and long-tail cast-on, CO 144 sts with
color 2 as the outer strand (over thumb) and color 1 for
the loops (over index finger). Divide sts evenly over 4 dpn,
slide slip knot off and join, being careful not to twist cast-
on row.

With color 1, work brim in seed st (Rnd 1: *K1, p1*; rep *
to * around. Rnd 2: *P1, k1*; rep * to * around) for 1 ¼ in
/ 3 cm. Change to larger dpn and charted pattern. Make
sure that the stranding does not pull in. After completing
charted rows, knit 1 rnd with color 1 and cut color 2.

TOP SHAPING K2tog at the center and end of each dpn
(= 8 sts dec per dec rnd) on every other round until 8 sts
remain. Cut yarn and weave in tails neatly on WS.

CABLES

Make this classic cabled hat a bit special by knitting with two shades of yellow. For a plain hat, work with a single color. In either case, the hat is a quick knit!

LEVEL OF DIFFICULTY Intermediate

YARN 6/2 wool yarn, 328 yds / 300 m per 100 g

YARN AMOUNTS color 1 yellow-green 1.9 oz/55 g, color 2 yellow 1.25 oz/35 g

NEEDLES set of 5 dpn US sizes 4 and 6 / 3.5 and 4 mm; cable needle

GAUGE 19 sts in stockinette on larger ndls = 4 in / 10 cm. Adjust needle sizes to obtain correct gauge if necessary.

FINISHED MEASUREMENTS circumference 21 in / 53 cm, length 8 ¾ in / 22 cm

With smaller needles and two strands of color 1 held together, CO 96 sts. Divide sts over 4 dpn and join, being careful not to twist cast-on row. Work in k2, p2 ribbing for 1 ¼ in / 3 cm = 9 rnds. Change to larger needles and 1 strand each of colors 1 and 2.

RND A *P2, k2, p2, k6*; rep * to * around. Work round A another 4 times.

RND B *P2, k2, p2, place 3 sts on cable needle in front of work, knit the next 3 sts and then knit 3 sts from cable ndl*; rep * to * around.

Work *rnd A 9 times, rnd B one time*; rep * to * 3 times.

TOP SHAPING *P1, k2tog, ssk, p1, k6*; rep * to * around. Repeat this decrease rnd on every 4nd rnd until 16 sts remain. Each dec rnd will have 2 fewer sts between the decreases.

The 2nd dec rnd is worked as *K2tog, ssk, k6*; rep * to * around.

The 3rd dec rnd: Use the last st from the previous rnd for the first dec *k2tog, ssk, k4*; rep * to * around.

Knit 1 rnd. On next rnd, k2tog around = 8 sts remain. Cut yarn and pull tail through rem sts but leave hole slightly open so that you can attach pompom.

POMPOM Wrap color 1 about 100 times around four fingers held together. Tie securely. Twist yarn around tip (see drawing). Trim pompom to 1 ¼ in / 3 cm. Sew securely to top of hat. See drawings. Weave in tails neatly on WS.

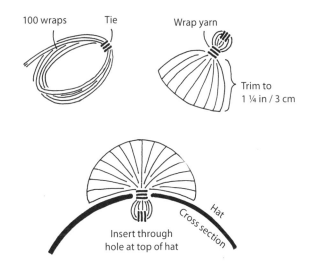

100 wraps   Tie   Wrap yarn

Trim to 1 ¼ in / 3 cm

Insert through hole at top of hat

Hat Cross section

RIBBED

This is the only hat in the book knit with three strands of yarn. It's extra heavy and warm. You can make this hat striped or a solid color.

LEVEL OF DIFFICULTY Easy

YARN tripled 6/2 wool yarn, 328 yds / 300 m per 100 g

YARN AMOUNTS color 1 dark blue 1 oz/30 g, color 2 blue 1 oz/30 g, color 3 light blue 1 oz/30 g

NEEDLES set of 5 dpn US size 8 / 5 mm

GAUGE 16 sts in stockinette = 4 in / 10 cm.
Adjust needle size to obtain correct gauge if necessary.

FINISHED MEASUREMENTS circumference 21 ¼ in / 54 cm, length 9 in / 23 cm

With one strand of each color held together, CO 84 sts. Divide sts over 4 dpn and join, being careful not to twist cast-on row. Work in k3, p3 ribbing for 6 in / 15 cm, or 8 in / 20 cm if you want an upturned brim (you might need more yarn in the latter case).

TOP SHAPING Decrease 14 sts evenly spaced around on every 4th rnd until 14 sts remain. Knit 1 rnd. K2tog around (= 7 sts rem). Cut yarn and pull through remaining sts. Weave in tails neatly on WS.

STARS

A traditional hat that's extra warm. When you pull the brim down, you'll find a couple of secret stripes in the ribbing!

LEVEL OF DIFFICULTY Experienced

YARN 6/2 wool yarn, 328 yds / 300 m per 100 g

YARN AMOUNTS color 1 black 1.25 oz/35 g, color 2 white 1.4 oz/40 g

NEEDLES 7 dpn or short circular US sizes 1.5 and 2.5 / 2.5 and 3 mm

GAUGE 27 sts in two-color pattern on larger ndls = 4 in / 10 cm. Adjust needle sizes to obtain correct gauge if necessary.

FINISHED MEASUREMENTS circumference 21 in / 53 cm, total length 11 in / 28 cm, length with brim upturned, 8 in / 20 cm

■ = knit with color 1
□ = knit with color 2

With color 1 and smaller ndls, CO 144 sts; join, being careful not to twist cast-on row. Knit 4 rnds in stockinette. Turn piece inside out so that the purl side is now facing out = rolled edge.

Change to color 2 and knit 1 rnd. Change to larger dpn (use 6 needles so that you have 1 dpn for each repeat). Work charted star pattern. Make sure that the knitting doesn't pull in! After completing pattern, change to smaller ndls and knit 1 rnd with color 2 and 1 rnd with color 1. Turn work inside out and work 7 rnds in stockinette with color 1 = welt. Change to color 2 and purl 1 rnd. Now work in k2/p2 ribbing in this color sequence: 1 ¼ in / 3 cm color 2, 2 rnds color 1, 2 rnds color 2, 2 rnds color 1, 1 ¼ in / 3 cm color 2. Knit 1 rnd. Change back to larger dpn and work first 13 rnds of crown pattern on chart.

CROWN SHAPING Dec 12 sts around as shown on chart: k1 with color 1, ssk with color 2, work in pattern across chart and knit the last 2 sts together with color 2. Rep the decreases on every 3rd rnd another 6 times and then dec on every rnd until 24 sts rem. With color 2, k2tog around. Cut yarn and pull through rem sts but leave hole slightly open so that you can attach pompom.

POMPOM Wrap color 1 25 times around 4 fingers held together. Tie as shown in drawing. Wrap yarn tightly near tip of bundle. Trim pompom to 1 ¼ in / 3 cm and then attach securely to top of hat. See drawings. Weave in all yarn tails on WS.

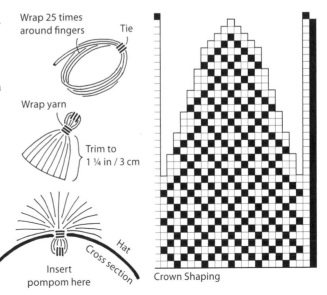

Wrap 25 times around fingers Tie

Wrap yarn

Trim to 1 ¼ in / 3 cm

Insert pompom here

Hat Cross section

Crown Shaping

FLAPS

The striped part is knitted first and then the hat is turned upside down so you can knit the ribbed ear flaps in the opposite direction. This hat keeps your ears really warm.

LEVEL OF DIFFICULTY Intermediate

YARN 6/2 wool yarn, 328 yds / 300 m per 100 g

YARN AMOUNTS color 1 gray 1.4 oz/40 g, color 2 blue .7 oz/20 g

NEEDLES set of 5 dpn US sizes 1.5 and 2.5 / 2.5 and 3 mm; stitch holders

GAUGE 26 sts in stockinette on larger needles = 4 in / 10 cm. Adjust needle sizes to obtain correct gauge if necessary.

FINISHED MEASUREMENTS circumference 21 in / 53 cm, length 8 ¾ in / 22 cm

With color 1 and larger ndls, CO 138 sts. Divide sts over 4 dpn 35-34-35-34; join, being careful not to twist cast-on row. Change to color 2 and work 3 rnds in stockinette. Alternate 3 rnds color 1, 3 rnds color 2 for striped pattern. Knit a total of 12 stripes = approx 3 ¼ in / 8.5 cm.

TOP SHAPING Continue striped pattern on crown. Decrease rnd: *K21, k2tog*; rep * to * around. Decrease on every other rnd until 12 sts remain, with 1 st less between decreases. Cut yarn and draw through rem sts; weave in tails neatly on WS.

RIBBING Remove color 1 strand from cast-on row and, with color 1 and smaller dpn, pick up and knit 138 sts.

Work in k1/p1 ribbing for 1 ¼ in / 3 cm. On the next rnd, BO 10 sts loosely, rib 31 sts and place these sts on a holder. BO 55 sts, work 31 sts in ribbing, BO 11 sts.

EAR FLAPS With smaller needles, work back and forth in ribbing over 31 sts for another 1 ½ in / 4 cm, always slipping the first st of every row purlwise. On next RS row, dec 1 st at each side on every other row. At beg of row, k1, p1, sl 1 knit st, p1, psso. Continue in ribbing across until 4 sts rem, k2tog, p1, k1. When 7 sts remain across, continue in ribbing with no further decreases for 6 in / 15 cm and then BO. Make the other ear flap the same way on the other set of 31 sts.

THE OTHER DIRECTION

The Other Direction is worked precisely as it sounds, that is, back and forth over two straight needles. It is quick and easy to knit in garter stitch with doubled yarn. You can also knit it in a single color.

LEVEL OF DIFFICULTY Easy

YARN doubled 6/2 wool yarn, 328 yds / 300 m per 100 g

YARN AMOUNTS color 1 black 1.4 oz/40 g, color 2 white 1.4 oz/40 g

NEEDLES straight needles US size 7 / 4.5 mm and one smaller size needle

GAUGE 20 sts in garter st = 4 in / 10 cm.
Adjust needle size to obtain correct gauge if necessary.

FINISHED MEASUREMENTS circumference 21 in / 53 cm, length 8 ¾ in / 22 cm

With 1 strand of each color and US 7 / 4.5 mm ndls, CO 43 sts. Knit 1 row. Always knit the first st on rows that will form lower edge of hat. Now shape hat with short rows: *k28; turn, slip 1st st and knit across rest of row. On the next row, k29 and then turn; sl 1, and knit rem sts. On every other row, knit 1 st more than previous short row until you are knitting across all 43 sts.* Work * to * a total of 5 times.

Now pick up and knit 43 sts from the cast-on row with the smaller needle. With WS facing, knit 1 st from hat together with 1 st from cast-on row, binding off at the same time (= three-needle bind-off). Cut yarn, leaving tail long enough to seam hat.

If you want a turned up brim, you need to begin with 55 sts. The first short row begins after working 40 sts instead of 28. You will also need more yarn, of course.

BONNET (HEAVY BONNET)

These bonnets are knitted like the classic baby bonnet but without the little point at the forehead. The bonnet knit with a single yarn is perfect for wearing under a hood or a liner for a hard hat. The striped heavy bonnet is knit with doubled yarn. Alternately you can knit it tweedy or with narrower stripes. Of course, it can be striped with single strands of yarn also because the number of rows in each section is evenly divided by 8 (= stripe repeat).

LEVEL OF DIFFICULTY Easy

YARN single (doubled) 6/2 wool yarn, 328 yds / 300 m per 100 g

YARN AMOUNTS 1.7 oz/50 g (color 1 red 1.25 oz/35 g, color 2 pink 1.25 oz/35 g)

NEEDLES straight needles US sizes 2.5 (7) / 3 (4.5) mm and one smaller size needle

GAUGE 27 (20) sts in garter st = 4 in / 10 cm.
Adjust needle sizes to obtain correct gauge if necessary.

FINISHED MEASUREMENTS circumference 20 ½ in / 52 cm, length 7 in / 18 cm

The bonnet is worked entirely in garter stitch.

With single strand of color 1, CO 50 sts (37 sts with doubled yarn) and knit 1 row. (For the stripes on the Heavy Bonnet: knit 2 rows with color 1 and then *4 rows color 2, 4 rows color 1*; rep * to * for remainder of bonnet. Carry unused color up side and twist colors on every other row.) Inc 1 st at the end of the first row by knitting into st below next-to-last st. Knit last st of row. On the next row, knit the first st and knit across until 3 sts rem, end k2tog, k1. On the following row, knit the first st and inc at the end of the row. Continue the same way, increasing only on one side and decreasing on

the other (except for sections 3 and 4).

FIRST SECTION Knit 56 (32) rows and make 28 (16) increases and the same number of decreases at the sides.

SECOND SECTION Knit 56 (32) rows but increase on the side where you had previously decreased and decrease at the side opposite earlier decreases.

THIRD SECTION Knit 28 (16) rows working only 14 (8) decreases on right side of piece until 36 (29) sts rem so that you do not make a little point.

FOURTH SECTION K28 (16) rows but only make 14 (8) increases on right side of piece until there are 50 (37) sts.

FIFTH SECTION As for first section.

SIXTH SECTION As for second section.

FINISHING With smaller needle, pick up and knit 50 (37) sts from cast-on row. With WS facing knit 1 st from last row of bonnet together with 1 st from cast-on row and bind off at the same time (= three-needle bind-off).
Sew the top of the bonnet edge to edge with RS facing. Make sure that the stripes match up.

STOCKING CAP

A classic stocking cap! Make it with wide or narrow stripes or just one color. Perhaps you'd like a contrast color for the ribbing? The I-cord tassel is knit with two needles.

LEVEL OF DIFFICULTY Easy

YARN 6/2 wool yarn, 328 yds / 300 m per 100 g

YARN AMOUNTS color 1 black 1 oz/30 g, color 2 white 1 oz/30 g

NEEDLES set of 5 dpn US sizes 1.5 and 2.5 / 2.5 and 3 mm

GAUGE 26 sts in stockinette on larger ndls = 4 in / 10 cm. Adjust needle sizes to obtain correct gauge if necessary.

FINISHED MEASUREMENTS circumference 21 in / 53 cm, length 11 ¾ in / 30 cm

TASSEL Wrap color 2 12 times around four fingers held together. Using yarn from I-cord, sew tassel to cord. Wrap color 2 around the tassel ⅜ in / 1 cm from end of cord and fasten. Trim tassel to 2 in / 5 cm length. See drawings.

With color 1 and smaller dpn, CO 136 sts and divided sts evenly over 4 dpn (= 34 sts per dpn). Join, being careful not to twist cast-on row. Work in k1, p1 ribbing for 1 ¼ in / 3 cm. Change to larger dpn and color 2. Work in stockinette, knitting 12 rnds for each wide stripe. Carry unused color up and twist colors on every 4th rnd. Knit a total of 4 stripes = approx 4 ¾ in / 12 cm.

TOP SHAPING On every other rnd, k2tog at the end of each dpn until 12 sts rem and then dec on every rnd until 4 sts rem.

I-CORD Place the 4 rem sts onto 1 larger size dpn and knit across; do not turn. Slide sts back to front of needle and knit. Tighten yarn across back as you start each new row. Continue until I-cord is 2 ½ in / 6 cm long; cut yarn and pull tail through rem sts.

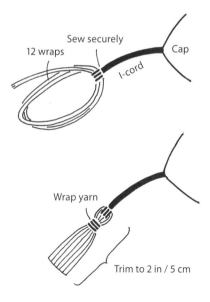

12 wraps Sew securely Cap I-cord

Wrap yarn Trim to 2 in / 5 cm

CHECKED HAT

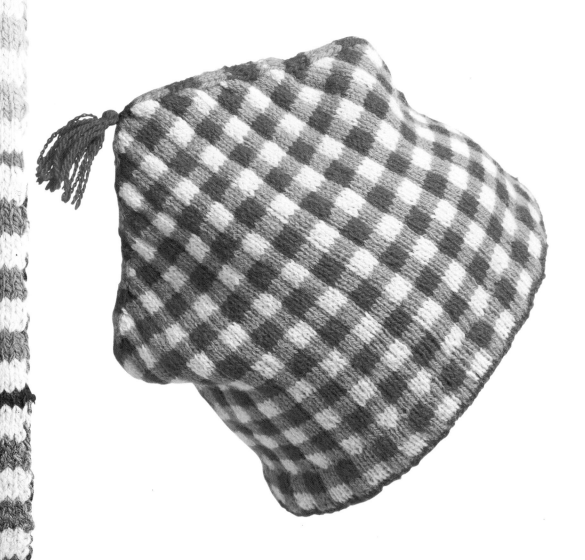

The traditional ski hat with a modern checked pattern.

LEVEL OF DIFFICULTY Experienced

YARN 6/2 wool yarn, 328 yds / 300 m per 100 g

YARN AMOUNTS color 1 white .7 oz/20 g, color 2 red .7 oz/20 g, color 3 pink 1 oz/30 g

NEEDLES set of 5 dpn US sizes 1.5 and 2.5 / 2.5 and 3 mm

GAUGE 27 sts in two-color stranded knitting on larger ndls = 4 in / 10 cm. Adjust needle sizes to obtain correct gauge if necessary.

FINISHED MEASUREMENTS circumference 21 in / 53 cm, length 9 ½ in / 24 cm

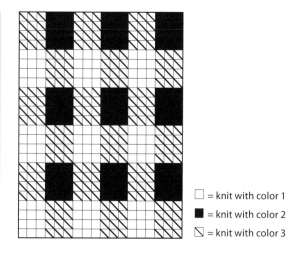

☐ = knit with color 1
■ = knit with color 2
◩ = knit with color 3

With color 1 and smaller dpn, CO 144 sts; divide sts evenly over 4 dpn (= 36 sts per dpn). Join, being careful not to twist cast-on row. Change to color 2 and work in stockinette for 9 rnds. Purl 1 rnd = fold line. Change to larger dpn and work in charted pattern for 8 rnds. Make sure that the knitting doesn't pull in. With smaller dpn, pick up every other st from cast-on row. On the next pattern rnd, turn edging at fold line and knit a cast-on row st together with every st from hat. Alternately, you could sew down facing when finishing hat, although it makes a less elastic edge. Work in pattern for a total of 44 rnds. On the next rnd, knit until 1 st rem. Move the 1st st from dpn 1 to dpn 4 and the 1st st from dpn 3 to dpn 2. This allows you to center the patterns for a smooth top shaping.

TOP SHAPING Knit together the 2 rem sts on dpn 4, k1 on ndl 1 and then ssk. Repeat these decreases over ndls 2 and 3. Dec the same way on every rnd. Make sure that the pattern in colors 2 and 3 continues as set on the side bands between the decrease lines. Dec until 12 sts remain. Cut yarn and pull through rem sts.

TASSEL Wrap color 2 12 times around four fingers held together. Tie around wraps and then wrap near tip of tassel. Trim tassel to 2 in / 5 cm length and sew securely to top of hat. See drawings.

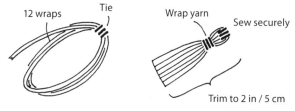

12 wraps Tie Wrap yarn Sew securely Trim to 2 in / 5 cm

STRIPES

Here's an everyday hat that fits softly over the head and comes down over your ears. The two-color stranded knitting makes the hat very warm and you can choose to make the whole hat with blocks or striped!

LEVEL OF DIFFICULTY Intermediate
YARN 6/2 wool yarn, 328 yds / 300 m per 100 g
YARN AMOUNTS color 1 black 1 oz/30 g, color 2 white 1 oz/30 g
NEEDLES set of 5 dpn US sizes 1.5 and 2.5 / 2.5 and 3 mm
GAUGE 27 sts in two-color stranded knitting on larger ndls = 4 in / 10 cm.
Adjust needle sizes to obtain correct gauge if necessary.
FINISHED MEASUREMENTS circumference 21 in / 53 cm, length 8 ¾ in / 22 cm

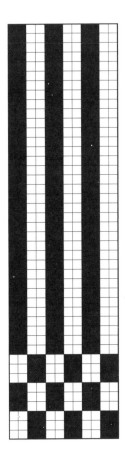

■ = knit with color 1
□ = knit with color 2

With color 1 and smaller dpn, CO 144 sts; divide sts evenly over 4 dpn (= 36 sts per dpn). Join, being careful not to twist cast-on row. Work in k2, p2 ribbing for 9 rnds in this color sequence: 3 rnds color 1, 3 rnds color 2, 3 rnds color 1. Change to larger dpn and work in charted pattern for 4 ¾ in / 12 cm. Make sure that the stranding doesn't pull in.

TOP SHAPING Continue in pattern as set. Dec 6 sts evenly spaced around (k21, *k2tog, k22*; rep * to * around and end k1). Dec on every other rnd 8 times and then on every rnd until 12 sts rem. There will be 1 less st between decreases on each dec rnd. Next, work k2tog around. Knit the rem 6 sts with color 1 for 8 rnds. Cut yarn and pull through rem sts. Weave in all tails neatly on WS.

BERET (HEAVY BERET)

Two berets in the classic size. All the stitches are increased at once after the ribbing. Maybe you'd prefer a tweed yarn for the heavy beret? The pattern goes around through the top shaping, sometimes there are 6 (4) purl stitches after the other but the pattern is such that it isn't noticeable.

LEVEL OF DIFFICULTY Intermediate

YARN single (doubled) 6/2 wool yarn, 328 yds / 300 m per 100 g

YARN AMOUNTS color 1 red 1.7 oz/50 g (white 2.5 oz/70 g), color 2 yellow-green 3 yds/meters (gray 6 yds/meters)

NEEDLES set of 5 dpn US sizes 1.5 and 2.5 / 2.5 and 3 mm (US 4 and 9 / 3.5 and 5.5 mm)

GAUGE 28 (16) sts in pattern on larger ndls = 4 in / 10 cm. Adjust needle sizes to obtain correct gauge if necessary.

FINISHED MEASUREMENTS diameter 10 ¾ in / 27 cm

Single yarn

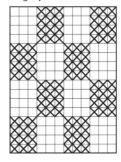

Doubled yarn

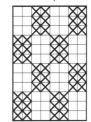

□ = knit

☒ = purl 1

Make a slip knot with both colors (two strands of each color) and place on smaller dpn for chosen size beret. Use long-tail cast-on to CO 108 (88) sts with color 2 over the thumb and color 1 over index finger (for loops on ndl). Remove slip knot. Join, being careful not to twist cast-on row. Work in k1, p1 ribbing with color 1 for 1 ¼ in / 3 cm. Knit 1 rnd and then change to larger dpn. On the next rnd, inc to 216 (132) sts with m1 between every st (between every other st). Work in charted pattern for 2 ½ in / 6 cm.

TOP SHAPING Place a strand of yarn around every dec as a marker, to make decrease lines more visible. Dec 12 sts evenly spaced around on every other (every 3rd) rnd until 24 sts rem. Work 1 rnd in pattern and then k2tog around. Work 1 rnd. Change to color 2 and smaller dpn and k2tog around. Knit the 6 rem sts for 8 rnds. Cut yarn and pull through rem sts. Weave in tails neatly on WS.

CUFFED BEANIE

Mistake stitch ribbing is worked back and forth with an odd number of stitches instead of in the round. It's an easy way to knit a textured pattern that looks like brioche.

LEVEL OF DIFFICULTY Easy

YARN 6/2 wool yarn, 328 yds / 300 m per 100 g

YARN AMOUNTS 2.1 oz/60 g

NEEDLES straight ndls US size 1.5 / 2.5 mm

GAUGE 39 sts in mistake st ribbing = 4 in / 10 cm.
Adjust needle size to obtain correct gauge if necessary.

FINISHED MEASUREMENTS circumference 21 in / 53 cm, length 9 ¾ in / 25 cm

CO 141 sts. Work in mistake stitch ribbing for 8 in / 20 cm.
Mistake stitch ribbing (all rows worked the same way):
Sl 1 purlwise, *k2, p2*; rep * to * across.

TOP SHAPING Sl 1 purlwise, k2, p2, k2, p2, k2, p1, *double dec with center st (= slip 2 sts knitwise at the same time, k1, psso), (p2, k2) 6 times, p1*; rep * to * another 3 times and end with k3tog, (p2, k2) 3 times, p2. On the next row, work in mistake rib, purling the decreased sts. Dec on every other row, making sure dec are stacked above each other. When 11 sts remain, work another 1 row. Cut yarn, leaving a long tail. Pull tail through rem sts and then seam cap through slipped edge sts.

SKULLCAP

The skullcap is just what it sounds like: a cap that doesn't cover the ears. This cap is lined so it's very warm. What about a striped skullcap?

LEVEL OF DIFFICULTY Intermediate

YARN 6/2 wool yarn, 328 yds / 300 m per 100 g

YARN AMOUNTS color 1 black .88 oz/25 g, color 2 red .88 oz/25 g

NEEDLES set of 5 dpn US sizes 1.5 and 2.5 / 2.5 and 3 mm

GAUGE 26 sts in stockinette on larger ndls = 4 in / 10 cm. Adjust needle sizes to obtain correct gauge if necessary.

FINISHED MEASUREMENTS circumference 21 ¾ in / 55 cm, length 7 in / 18 cm

TOP SHAPING Dec 13 sts evenly spaced around (*K9 k2tog; rep * to * around). Knit 2 rnds. Next dec rnd, *K8, k2tog*; rep * to * around. Dec the same way (with 1 less st between decreases each time) on every 3rd rnd until 13 sts rem. K2tog around, end k1.

Change to color 1 and knit the rem 7 sts for 8 rnds. Cut yarn and pull tail through rem sts. Weave in all tails neatly on WS.

With color 1 and smaller dpn, CO 143 sts; divide sts over 4 dpn. Join, being careful not to twist cast-on row. Work in stockinette for 2 ¾ in / 7 cm. Turn so that piece is inside out and WS is facing. Work in stockinette for 4 rnds. Change to larger dpn and knit another 4 rnds = total of 8 rnds for wide rolled edge. Turn cap right side out, change to color 2 and continue in stockinette for 2 ¾ in / 7 cm. With smaller dpn and WS facing, pick up every other st from cast-on row. Change to color 1 and join lining by knitting 1 cast-on st together with every other cap st around.

Turn cap so RS is facing and knit 4 rnds with color 1 and larger dpn = welt. Turn, change to color 2 and knit 3 rnds.

mittens
BAGGY

Here's an easy basic mitten. The lice design and the extra long cuffs make them nice and warm. Baggy is knitted with a size smaller needle than for the hat of the same name so that the mittens will be tighter and more durable.

LEVEL OF DIFFICULTY Intermediate

YARN 6/2 wool yarn, 328 yds / 300 m per 100 g

YARN AMOUNTS for one pair: color 1 black 1.4 oz/40 g, color 2 white .7 oz/20 g

NEEDLES set of 5 dpn US sizes 0 and 1.5 / 2 and 2.5 mm

GAUGE 29 sts in pattern on larger ndls = 4 in / 10 cm. Adjust needle sizes to obtain correct gauge if necessary.

FINISHED MEASUREMENTS width 3 ¾ in / 9.5 cm, length 13 in / 33 cm

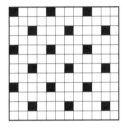

☐ = knit with color 1
■ = knit with color 2

With color 1 and smaller dpn, CO 56 sts. Divide sts evenly over 4 dpn (= 14 sts per dpn), and join being careful not to twist cast-on row. Work around in k2, p2 ribbing for 2 ¾ in / 7 cm. Change to color 2 and continue in ribbing for another 2 ¾ in / 7 cm.

Change to larger dpn and charted pattern; add color 1. Make sure that the stranding of color 2 doesn't pull in knitting. Work in pattern for 2 ½ in / 6 cm, ending with a two-color rnd. With smooth contrast color waste yarn, work 11 sts at beginning of ndl 3 (= thumbhole), slide those 11 sts back to left ndl, and continue in pattern until patterned section is a total of 6 ¾ in / 17 cm long.

TOP SHAPING Ssk at beg of ndls 1 and 3 and k2tog at end of ndls 2 and 4 on every rnd until 8 sts remain. Cut yarn and pull through rem sts.

THUMB (STRAIGHT) Remove waste yarn and, with larger dpn, pick up 24 sts around thumbhole. Work in pattern and shape top as for hand when thumb is 2 ½ in / 6 cm long. Cut yarn.

SECOND MITTEN Work as for first mitten but place thumbhole over the last 11 sts of ndl 2.

39

SCRAPS (HEAVY SCRAPS)

The welts on the Scraps mitten cuffs will fill your sleeves so no cold air can get in. Of course, you are welcome to knit a ribbed cuff instead. The fingers are fun to knit because they go so fast. The little finger is aligned with the other fingers here because of the stripe. If you want to make a Scraps mitten, keep in mind that gloves fit the hand more tightly than mittens.

LEVEL OF DIFFICULTY Easy

YARN single (doubled) 6/2 wool yarn, 328 yds / 300 m per 100 g
Yarn amounts for one pair: color 1 gray 1.25 oz/35 g (black 1.75 oz/50 g), color 2 white .88 oz/25 g (blue 1.4 oz/40 g)

NEEDLES set of 5 dpn US sizes 1.5 (6) / 2.5 (4) mm; stitch holders

GAUGE 28 (19) sts in stockinette = 4 in / 10 cm.
Adjust needle size to obtain correct gauge if necessary.

FINISHED MEASUREMENTS width 3 ¼ (4) in / 8.5 (10) cm, length when stretched 13 ¾ (11 ¾) in / 33 (30) cm

The entire mitten is knit in stockinette in 6- (5-) row wide stripes (excluding the cast-on row). The cuff stripes in color 1 have purl sts facing out and the work is turned inside out with each color change. Before turning work for the color change between colors 2 and 1, work the first rnd of color 1. With color 1, CO 48 sts with single strand of yarn (38 sts with doubled yarn). Divide sts over 4 dpn and join, being careful not to twist cast-on row. Work as described above for 5 (4) welts. Next, work 5 (4) stripes in stockinette = 2 ¾ (2 ½) in / 7 (6.5) cm. With smooth contrast color waste yarn, knit the first 10 (8) sts on ndl 1 and then slide them back to left ndl and continue in pattern (= thumbhole).

Gloves with single strand of yarn

Work another 4 stripes = 2 ¼ in / 5.5 cm.

Note: When shaping finger tips, work out decreases as evenly as possible. In some cases, you will have an extra st or two at the end of the round.

Place all the sts on a holder except for the first 7 sts of ndl 1 and the last 7 sts of ndl 4 which will be used for the index finger.

INDEX FINGER (17 STS) With color 1 and 3 dpn, knit 7 + 7 sts and, on the first rnd, CO 3 sts at base of middle finger. Knit around until finger is 2 ¾ in / 7 cm long and then shape tip: *K2, k2tog; rep from * around. On the next rnd, *k1, k2tog; rep from * around. On the last rnd, k2tog around. Cut yarn and pull through rem sts.

MIDDLE FINGER (18 STS) Place 6 sts from each side of hand onto dpn and pick up and knit 3 sts at base of index finger. On the first rnd, with color 1,

CO 3 sts at ring finger and knit around on 3 dpn. When finger measures 3 in / 7.5 cm, shape tip as for index finger.

RING FINGER (18 STS) Work as for middle finger but only until same length as index finger.

LITTLE FINGER (14 STS) Place remaining sts on 3 dpn and pick up and knit 4 sts at base of ring finger. When little finger is 2 in / 5 cm long, shape tip as for index finger.

THUMB (STRAIGHT) Remove waste yarn and pick up 22 sts around thumbhole and divide over 4 dpn. With color 1, knit around, decreasing 2 sts evenly spaced on 10th rnd. When thumb measures 2 ½ in / 6 cm, shape tip as for index finger.

SECOND GLOVE Work as for first with thumbhole placed over last 10 sts of ndl 4.

Mittens with doubled yarn

Work in stripe pattern until stockinette section is 6 ¾ in / 17 cm long.

TOP SHAPING Ssk at beg of ndls 1 and 3 and k2tog at end of ndls 2 and 4 on every rnd until 6 sts rem. Cut yarn and pull through remaining sts.

THUMB (STRAIGHT) Remove waste yarn and pick up 18 sts around thumbhole; divide onto 4 dpn and join. Work in stripes for 2 ½ in / 6 cm and then shape as for mitten top. Cut yarn and pull through rem sts.

SECOND MITTEN Work as for first with thumbhole placed over the last 8 sts of ndl 4.

SPRUCE

Thumbhole

☐ = knit with color 1
■ = knit with color 2

The spruce pattern looks a bit different on the mittens than on the hat. The mittens will be easier to knit if you work with 6 double-pointed needles so that you have 1 pattern repeat on each needle. The thumb and cuff are soft and easy to knit in seed stitch.

LEVEL OF DIFFICULTY Intermediate
YARN 6/2 wool yarn, 328 yds / 300 m per 100 g
YARN AMOUNTS for one pair: color 1 black 1.4 oz/40 g, color 2 yellow-green 1 oz/30 g
NEEDLES set of 6 dpn US sizes 0 and 1.5 / 2 and 2.5 mm
GAUGE 29 sts in pattern on larger ndls = 4 in / 10 cm.
Adjust needle sizes to obtain correct gauge if necessary.
FINISHED MEASUREMENTS width 3 ¾ in / 9.5 cm, length 11 in / 28 cm

Make a slip knot loop with both colors and place on smaller size dpn. With long-tail method, CO 44 sts with color 2 over the thumb and color 1 over the index finger (for loops on ndl). Remove slip knot. Divide sts over 4 dpn and join, being careful not to twist cast-on row. With color 1, work in seed st (*k1, p1*; rep * to * around. On the next rnd, *p1, k1*; rep * to * around) for 3 ¼ in / 8 cm. Change to larger ndls and knit 1 rnd. On the next rnd, increase 16 sts evenly spaced around: *m1, k3*; rep * to * around and end with m1.

Now work in charted pattern with sts divided over 5 dpn (one for each repeat to make the knitting easier). Make sure that the stranding doesn't pull in the knitting.

After working 24 pattern rnds, knit the 12 thumbhole sts with smooth, contrast color waste yarn (see placement on chart). Move the 12 sts back to left needle and continue in pattern until spruce pattern is a total of 6 ¾ in / 17 cm long. Divide sts over 4 dpn.

TOP SHAPING Work the bands at each side of the mitten top in color 1 (= first st on ndls 1 and 3 and last st on ndls 2 and 4). Dec with ssk at beginning of ndls 1 and 3 and k2tog at end of ndls 2 and 4. Decrease on every rnd until 8 sts remain. Cut yarn and pull through rem sts.

THUMB (STRAIGHT) Remove waste yarn and, with smaller dpn, pick up 26 sts around thumbhole. Knit 1 rnd with color 1. Work in seed st as for cuff, decreasing 1 st at each side of thumb on first rnd (= 24 sts rem). When thumb is 2 ¼ in / 5.5 cm long, begin shaping tip. *Work 2 sts in pattern and then 2 tog*; rep * to * around. Work 2 rnds without shaping (with knit over purl and purl over knit). On the next rnd, work 1 st in pattern and then 2 tog (knit or purl as appropriate); rep * to * around. Work 1 rnd without decreasing and then k2tog around. Cut yarn and pull through rem sts.

SECOND MITTEN Work as for first with thumbhole placed over the last 12 sts of ndl 4.

CABLES

The cable makes the mitten more elastic so it fits better over your hand. You won't need an extra needle for this cable pattern.

LEVEL OF DIFFICULTY Intermediate

YARN doubled 6/2 wool yarn, 328 yds / 300 m per 100 g

YARN AMOUNTS for one pair: color 1 red 1.75 oz/50 g, color 2 deep pink 1 oz/30 g

NEEDLES set of 5 dpn US sizes 4 and 6 / 3.5 and 4 mm

GAUGE 20 sts in stockinette on larger ndls = 4 in / 10 cm. Adjust needle sizes to obtain correct gauge if necessary.

FINISHED MEASUREMENTS WIDTH 3 ¾ in / 9.5 cm, length 10 ¾ in / 27 cm

With 2 strands of color 1 held together and smaller dpn, CO 40 sts. Divide sts over 4 dpn and join, being careful not to twist cast-on row. Work in ribbing: K1, *p2, k2*; rep * to * around and end with k1 (instead of k2). The ribbing is set up so that the cable will be centered. Continue in ribbing as set for 3 ¼ in / 8 cm. Change to larger dpn and 1 strand of each color held together (cut extra strand of color 1 used for cuffs).

Work 5 rnds in pattern: K5, p2, k6, p2, and then knit to end of rnd.

On the 6th rnd, turn cable: K5, p2, hold next 3 sts in front (or place 3 sts onto cable needle and hold in front) and then k3 from ndl 2. Place the 3 sts held in front onto ndl 2 and knit, p2 and then knit rem sts of rnd. Repeat this cable turn on every 10th rnd another 5 times.

When mitten is 2 ½ in / 6.5 cm past ribbing, knit the first 8 sts on ndl 3 with a smooth contrast color waste yarn for thumbhole. Slide the 8 sts back to left ndl and continue in pattern until stockinette/ cable pattern is a total of 6 ¾ in / 17 cm long.

TOP SHAPING Work ssk at beg of ndls 1 and 3 and k2tog at end of ndls 2 and 4 on every rnd until 8 sts remain. Cut yarn and pull through remaining sts.

THUMB (STRAIGHT) Remove waste yarn and, with larger ndls, pick up 18 sts around thumbhole. Work around in stockinette and, when thumb is 2 ⅜ in / 6 cm long, shape tip as for top of mitten. When 6 sts remain, cut yarn and pull through rem sts.

SECOND MITTEN Work as for first with thumbhole placed over the last 8 sts of ndl 4.

FINISHING Turn mittens inside and brush (see Read this Section First).

TWEED

The heaviest mittens in the book are quick to knit with three strands of yarn. Make them tweedy or a single color. Brushing the inside makes the mittens even warmer.

LEVEL OF DIFFICULTY Easy

YARN tripled 6/2 wool yarn, 328 yds / 300 m per 100 g

YARN AMOUNTS for one pair: color 1 black 1.25 oz/35 g, color 2 gray 1.25 oz/35 g, color 3 white 1.25 oz/35 g

NEEDLES set of 5 dpn US sizes 6 and 8 / 4 and 5 mm

GAUGE 16 sts in pattern on larger ndls = 4 in / 10 cm. Adjust needle sizes to obtain correct gauge if necessary.

FINISHED MEASUREMENTS width 4 in / 10 cm, length 11 in / 28 cm

With smaller ndls and 1 strand of each color held together, CO 32 sts. Divide sts over 4 dpn and join, being careful not to twist cast-on row. Work around in k2, p2 ribbing for 3 ¼ in / 8 cm. Change to larger dpn and work in stockinette for 2 ½ in / 6.5 cm. With smooth contrast color waste yarn, knit the first 7 sts on ndl 3 for thumbhole. Slide the 7 sts back to left ndl and continue in pattern until stockinette part of mitten is 6 ¾ in / 17 cm long.

TOP SHAPING Work ssk at beg of ndls 1 and 3 and k2tog at end of ndls 2 and 4 on every rnd until 8 sts remain. Cut yarn and pull through remaining sts.

THUMB (STRAIGHT) Remove waste yarn and, with larger ndls, pick up 16 sts around thumbhole. Work around in stockinette and, when thumb is 2 ⅜ in / 6 cm long, shape tip as for top of mitten. When 4 sts remain, cut yarn and pull through rem sts.

SECOND MITTEN Work as for first with thumbhole placed over the last 7 sts of ndl 2.

FINISHING Turn mittens inside and brush (see Read this Section First).

FLAPS

A fine and supple mitten for anyone with narrow hands!
The thumb gusset helps the mitten fit particularly well at
the wrist.

LEVEL OF DIFFICULTY Easy

YARN 6/2 wool yarn, 328 yds / 300 m per 100 g

YARN AMOUNTS for one pair: color 1 gray 1 oz/30 g, color 2 red .88 oz/20 g

NEEDLES set of 5 dpn US sizes 0 and 1.5 / 2 and 2.5

GAUGE 28 sts in stockinette on larger ndls = 4 in / 10 cm. Adjust needle sizes to obtain correct gauge if necessary.

FINISHED MEASUREMENTS width 3 ¾ in / 9.5 cm, length 11 in / 28 cm

With color 1 and smaller dpn, CO 44 sts. Divide sts over 4 dpn and join, being careful not to twist cast-on row. Work in k1, p1 ribbing for 3 ¼ in / 8 cm.
Change to larger dpn and add color 2. The stripe pattern is worked in stockinette with each stripe 3 rnds wide. Begin with color 2 and knit 2 rnds.

THUMB GUSSET K1, m1, k1, m1, knit to end of rnd. Work this inc on every 6th rnd a total of 5 times; there will be 2 more sts between increases each time. Now divide the sts 14-13-14-13. When 10 stripes have been completed, knit the 11 thumb gusset sts with a smooth contrast color waste yarn. Slide these 11 sts back to left ndl and continue in pattern until there are a total of 25 stripes = 6 ¾ in / 17 cm.

TOP SHAPING Work ssk at beg of ndls 1 and 3 and k2tog at end of ndls 2 and 4 on every rnd until 6 sts remain. Cut yarn and pull through remaining sts.

THUMB Remove waste yarn and, with larger ndls, pick up 24 sts around thumbhole. Work 9 stripes = 2 ⅜ in / 6 cm and then shape tip as for top of mitten. When 8 sts remain, cut yarn and pull through rem sts.

SECOND MITTEN Work as for first, beginning thumb gusset on the 4th ndl: K9, m1, k1, m1, k1.

BONNET (HEAVY BONNET)

The gloves fit well because they have a thumb gusset, lower little finger, and a garter stitch cuff. The mittens also fit well even though they are knitted with doubled yarn.

LEVEL OF DIFFICULTY Intermediate

YARN single (doubled) 6/2 wool yarn, 328 yds / 300 m per 100 g

YARN AMOUNTS for one pair: color 1 yellow-green 1.4 oz/40 g (red 1.75 oz/50 g), color 2 red .35 oz/10 g (white 1 oz/30 g)

NEEDLES straight ndls and set of 5 dpn US size 1.5 (6) / 2.5 (4) mm; stitch holders

GAUGE 28 (19) sts in stockinette on dpn = 4 in / 10 cm. Adjust needle size to obtain correct gauge if necessary.

FINISHED MEASUREMENTS width 3 ¼ (4) in / 8.5 (10) cm, length 10 ¾ in / (11) in / 27 (28) cm

With smaller straight ndls and color 1, CO 41 sts with single strand (CO 33 sts with doubled yarn) work back and forth in garter stitch for 2 ¾ in / 7 cm as follows: change to color 2 after 1 row and then knit 2-row-wide stripes, with the last stripe in color 1 (3 ¼ in / 8 cm for single color). Change to dpn and color 2 with single yarn (1 strand each colors 1 and 2) and stockinette. Make sure that the right side of the cast-on row is on the RS. Now join by knitting the first st on ndl 1 with the last st on ndl 4 together and then knit 4 (1) rnds.

THUMB GUSSET K1, m1, k2, m1, knit to end of rnd. Work this inc on every 7th rnd a total of 4 (3) times; there will be 2 more sts between increases each time. Now divide the sts 12-12-12-12 (10-9-10-9). When stockinette section is 2 ½ in / 6.5 cm long, knit the 10 (8) thumb gusset sts with a smooth contrast color waste yarn. Slide these 10 (8) sts back to left ndl.

Gloves with single strand of yarn

Continue in stockinette until stockinette section is 4 in / 10 cm long. Place the last 5 sts of ndl 2 and the first 5 sts of ndl 3 on stitch holders. Knit 4 rnds on rem sts, casting on 3 sts between the 2nd and 3rd ndls on the first rnd. Place all sts except for the first 7 sts of ndl 1 and the last 7 sts of ndl 4 onto holders. The 14 rem sts are for the index finger.

Note: When shaping finger tips, work out decreases as evenly as possible. In some cases, you will have an extra st or two at the end of the round.

INDEX FINGER (17 STS) Divide the 7 + 7 sts over 3 dpn and, on the first rnd, CO 3 sts at base of middle finger. Knit around until finger is 2 ¾ in / 7 cm long and then shape tip: *K2, k2tog; rep from * around. On the next rnd, *k1, k2tog; rep from * around. On the last rnd, k2tog around. Cut yarn and pull through rem sts.

RING FINGER (18 STS) Divide the 15 sts nearest little finger onto 3 dpn and CO 3 sts at base of middle finger. Work as for index finger.

MIDDLE FINGER (18 STS) Place 6 sts from each side of hand onto 3 dpn and pick up and knit 3 sts at base of index finger and 3 sts at base of ring finger. When finger measures 3 in / 7.5 cm, shape tip as for index finger.

LITTLE FINGER (14 STS) Place 10 sts on 3 dpn and pick up and knit 4 sts at base of ring finger. When little finger is 2 in / 5 cm long, shape tip as for index finger.

THUMB Remove waste yarn and pick up 22 sts around thumbhole and divide over 4 dpn. Knit around, decreasing 1 st at each side on 5th rnd. When thumb is 2 ⅜ in / 6 cm long, shape tip as for index finger.

SECOND GLOVE Work as for first, beginning thumb gusset on the 4th ndl: K7, m1, k2, m1, k1.

FINISHING With RS facing, seam cuffs with mattress stitch.

Mitten with doubled yarn

Work until stockinette section is 6 ¾ in / 17 cm long.

TOP SHAPING Work ssk at beg of ndls 1 and 3 and k2tog at end of ndls 2 and 4 on every rnd until 6 sts remain. Cut yarn and pull through remaining sts.

THUMB Remove waste yarn and, with larger ndls, pick up 18 sts around thumbhole. When thumb is 2 ⅜ in / 6 cm long, shape tip as for top of mitten. When 6 sts remain, cut yarn and pull through rem sts.

SECOND MITTEN Work as for first, beginning thumb gusset on the 4th ndl: K5, m1, k2, m1, k1.

FINISHING With RS facing, seam cuffs with mattress stitch. Turn mittens inside out and brush (see Read this Section First).

STOCKING (HEAVY STOCKING)

This truly is a basic mitten! The side gusset makes plenty of room for the lower part of the hand without feeling bulky. The right and left mittens are knitted exactly the same way. You can make narrower stripes or use a single color. Maybe the thicker mitten could be tweedy? Don't forget to brush the insides.

LEVEL OF DIFFICULTY Easy
YARN single (doubled) 6/2 wool yarn, 328 yds / 300 m per 100 g
YARN AMOUNTS for one pair: color 1 red 1.4 oz/40 g (black 2.1 oz/60 g), color 2 white .88 oz/20 g (red 1 oz/30 g)
NEEDLES set of 5 dpn US sizes 0 and 1.5 (4 and 6) / 2 and 2.5 (3.5 and 4) mm
GAUGE 28 (19) sts in stockinette on larger ndls = 4 in / 10 cm.
Adjust needle sizes to obtain correct gauge if necessary.
FINISHED MEASUREMENTS width 3 ¾ (4) in / 9.5 (10) cm, length 10 ¾ (10 ¾) in / 27 (27) cm

With smaller ndls and color 1, CO 54 sts with single yarn (with doubled yarn, CO 38 sts). Divide sts over 4 dpn and join, being careful not to twist cast-on row. Work around in k1, p1 ribbing for 3 ¼ in / 8 cm. Change to larger dpn and color 2 with single (double) yarn and work in 12-(8)-row-wide stockinette stripes. On every 4th rnd, catch unused color. Work 5 (3) rnds and then begin thumb gusset.

SIDE THUMB GUSSET When 1 st rem on ndl 2, m1 and then knit last st. On ndl 3, k1, m1. Repeat this inc on every other rnd; each time there will be 2 more sts between increases. Work increase a total of 11 (8) times.

When stockinette section is 2 ½ in / 6.5 in long (2 ½ stripes), place the 24 (18) sts of thumb gusset on a stitch holder. CO 2 sts over gap on the next rnd. Continue in stockinette stripes until 6 ¾ in / 17 cm past ribbing.

TOP SHAPING Work ssk at beg of ndls 1 and 3 and k2tog at end of ndls 2 and 4 on every rnd until 6 sts remain. Cut yarn and pull through remaining sts.

THUMB Place the 24 (18) sts onto dpn and pick up and knit 2 sts next to hand. Knit 1 rnd. On the next rnd, knit each of the 2 extra sts together with neighboring thumb sts. When thumb measures 1 ¾ in / 4.5 cm, begin shaping tip. *K2, k2tog; rep from * around. Knit 2 (1) rnds without shaping. Next rnd: *K1, k2tog; rep from * around. Knit 1 rnd. Last rnd: K2tog around. Cut yarn and pull through rem sts.

SECOND MITTEN Work as for first.

Turn heavy mittens inside out and brush (see Read this Section First).

CHECKED

The Checked gloves place the little fingers a bit lower on the hand and feature patterned cuffs for extra warmth around the wrist. You could make the cuffs with lengthwise stripes or in a lice pattern.

LEVEL OF DIFFICULTY Experienced
Yarn 6/2 wool yarn, 328 yds / 300 m per 100 g

YARN amounts for one pair: color 1 white .7 oz/20 g, color 2 blue 1.4 oz/40 g, color 3 light blue .35 oz/10 g

NEEDLES set of 5 dpn US sizes 0, 1.5 and 2.5 / 2, 2.5 and 3 mm

GAUGE 28 sts in stockinette on US 1.5 / 2.5 mm = 4 in / 10 cm. Adjust needle sizes to obtain correct gauge if necessary.

FINISHED MEASUREMENTS width 3 ¼ in / 8.5 cm, length 10 ¾ in / 27 cm (total 13 ¼ in / 33.5 cm)

With color 2 and dpn US 1.5 / 2.5 mm, CO 48 sts. Divide sts over 4 dpn and join, being careful not to twist cast-on row. Knit 5 rnds in stockinette. Turn work inside out so that the purl side is now on the outside = rolled edge. Change to US 2.5 / 3 mm dpn and charted pattern. Make sure that the strands don't pull in the knitting. After completing charted rows, change to US 1.5 / 2.5 mm ndls and color 2; knit 1 rnd. Turn and knit 7 rnds = welt. Change to US 0 / 2 mm dpn and color 1 and purl 1 rnd. Work in k3, p3 ribbing for 2 ½ in / 6.5 cm. Change to US 1.5 / 2.5 mm dpn and color 2 and knit 5 rnds.

SIDE THUMB GUSSET When 1 st rem on ndl 2, m1 and then k1; k1 on ndl 3 and then m1. Work this inc on every other rnd a total of 10 times; there will be 2 more sts between increases each time. When stockinette section is 2 ½ in / 6.5 cm long, place the 22 thumb gusset sts on a holder.

On the next rnd, CO 2 sts over gap. Continue until stockinette section measures 4 in / 10 cm. Knit the first 5 sts on ndl 1 and place them on a holder. Finish rnd except for the last 5 sts on ndl 4 and place those 5 sts on a holder. CO 3 sts between the 4th and 1st ndls and knit 4 rnds. Place all sts except for the 15 sts nearest little finger on holders. The rem 15 sts form the ring finger.

Note: When shaping finger tips, work out decreases as evenly as possible. In some cases, you will have an extra st or two at the end of the round.

RING FINGER (18 STS) Divide the 15 sts nearest little finger onto 3 dpn and, on the first rnd, CO 3 sts at base of middle finger. Knit around until finger is 2 ¾ in / 7 cm long and then shape tip: *K2, k2tog; rep from * around. On the

next rnd, *k1, k2tog; rep from * around. On the last rnd, k2tog around. Cut yarn and pull through rem sts.

INDEX FINGER (17 STS) Place 7 + 7 sts onto 3 dpn and, on the first rnd, CO 3 sts at base of middle finger. When finger is 2 ¾ in / 7 cm long, shape as for ring finger.

MIDDLE FINGER (18 STS) Place 6 sts from each side of hand onto 3 dpn and pick up and knit 3 sts at base of index finger and 3 sts at base of ring finger. When finger is 3 in / 7.5 cm long, shape tip as for ring finger.

LITTLE FINGER (14 STS) Place 10 sts on 3 dpn and pick up and knit 4 sts at base of ring finger. When little finger is 2 in / 5 cm long, shape tip as for ring finger.

THUMB Place 22 thumb sts onto 3 dpn, pick up and knit 2 sts at hand and knit 4 rnds. On the next rnd, knit each of the 2 extra sts together with neighboring thumb sts and then decrease another 2 sts on the following rnd = 20 sts. When thumb is 2 ¼ in / 5.15 cm long, shape tip as for ring finger.

SECOND GLOVE Work as for first.

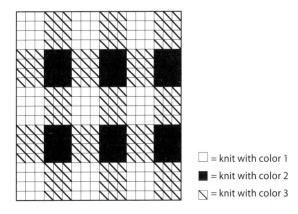

☐ = knit with color 1
■ = knit with color 2
◩ = knit with color 3

BLOCKS

Knitting with two strands of yarn that twist around each other on the back makes the mittens warm and firm. The knitting takes some time but the result will be a fine and long-lasting pair of mittens.

LEVEL OF DIFFICULTY Experienced
YARN 6/2 wool yarn, 328 yds / 300 m per 100 g
YARN AMOUNTS color 1 red 1 oz/30 g, color 2 white 1 oz/30 g
NEEDLES straight ndls US size 0 / 2 mm; set of 5 dpn US sizes 1.5 and 2.5 / 2.5 and 3 mm; stitch holders
GAUGE 29 sts in two-color pattern on US 2.5 / 3 mm ndls = 4 in / 10 cm. Adjust needle sizes to obtain correct gauge if necessary.
FINISHED MEASUREMENTS width 3 ½ in / 9 cm, length 11 in / 28 cm

With color 1 and straight ndls, CO 52 sts. Work back and forth in garter st (knit every row) as follows: 1 row color 1, 2 rows color 2, and 2 rows color 1.

Change to smaller dpn, divide sts onto 4 dpn, and join to work in the round. Work charted 1/1 stripe pattern. Twist the yarns around each other in one direction for the first half of the round and in the opposite direction for rest of rnd. Make sure you don't pull the yarn too tightly! Work in stripe pattern for 3 ½ in / 9 cm. Change to larger dpn and begin block pattern and thumb gusset following the chart.

SIDE THUMB GUSSET Inc for the thumb gusset with m1 by lifting strands between the 11th and 12th sts of ndl 2 and the 1st and 2nd sts of ndl 3. Inc on every other rnd, with 2 more sts between increases each time. Inc a total of 9 times (see chart). After completing the 20 gusset rnds, place 21 sts for thumb onto stitch holder. On the next rnd, CO 3 sts over the gap. Work until block pattern measures 6 ¾ in / 17 cm.

TOP SHAPING The 3 sts cast on over the thumbhole and the corresponding 3 sts on ndls 1 and 4 will form a band at each side of the mitten. Use color 2 for the center st and color 1 for outer sts of each band. Dec between the bands with k2tog in color 1, k1 with color 2 after right side band and, before next band, ssk with color 1. Repeat this dec on each side of mitten on every rnd until 8 sts rem. Cut yarn and pull tail through rem sts.

THUMB Place the 21 thumb sts onto larger dpn and pick up and knit 3 sts above thumbhole. Work around in block pattern for 18 rnds. Now shape tip: *k2, k2tog; rep from * around. Work 1 rnd without dec. On next rnd,*k1, k2tog; rep from * around. Next rnd: K2tog around. Cut yarn

and pull tail through rem sts. Seam garter stitch edge and weave in all tails on WS.

SECOND MITTEN Work as for first.

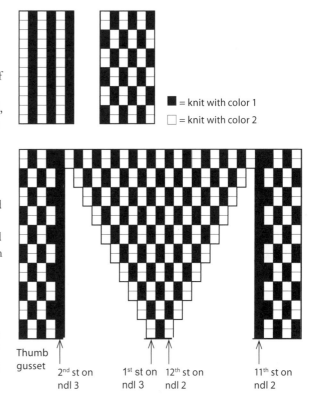

= knit with color 1
= knit with color 2

Thumb gusset

2nd st on ndl 3   1st st on ndl 3   12th st on ndl 2   11th st on ndl 2

WRIST WARMERS

Wrist warmers are easily knit and very practical. Your whole body will be warmed by them. With a wide choice of colors and patterns you can match any garment. Choose any mitten cuff pattern in the book and make just the cuff as long as you want. I've chosen a few as examples. Some are adapted from hat brims.

LEVEL OF DIFFICULTY Easy
YARN 6/2 wool yarn, 328 yds / 300 m per 100 g
YARN AMOUNTS for one pair: .88 oz/25 g single strand of yarn, 1.75 oz/50 g doubled yarn

Ribbing

As for the Cables (Tweed) Mittens: With doubled (tripled) yarn and dpn US 4 (6), CO 40 (32) sts; join, being careful not to twist cast-on row. Work in k2, p2 ribbing for 4 ¾ in / 12 cm and then bind off.

Garter Stitch

As for the Heavy Bonnet (The Other Direction hat): With straight ndls US 7 / 4.5 mm and doubled yarn in one color (two colors), CO 30 (24) sts = 6 (4 ¾) in / 15 (12) cm. Knit a total of 64 rows in garter stitch, changing colors for the stripes, first after the 5th row and then after every 4th row. Finishing: With a smaller needle, pick up 30 (24) sts from the cast-on row. With WS facing, knit 1 from last row together with 1 cast-on row stitch and bind off at the same time (= three-needle bind-off).

Mistake Stitch Ribbing

As for Cuffed Beanie: With straight ndls US 1.5 (4) / 2.5 (3.5) mm and single (doubled) yarn, CO 57 (41) sts. All rows are worked the same way: Slip the first st purlwise, *k2, p2*; rep * to * across. When piece is 4 ¾ (6) in / 12 (15) cm long, bind off.

Welts

As for Scraps (Heavy Scraps) mittens: With dpn US 1.5 / 2.5 mm (US 6 / 4 mm) and single (doubled) yarn, CO 48 (38) sts; join, being careful not to twist cast-on row. Work 6- (5-) row wide stockinette stripes. Turn work at each color change, always knitting the first rnd on every other color change before turning. Work 13 (11) stripes = 7 (6) welts. Bind off.

STARS

I found the original for this classic mitten many years ago in my grand-mother's cupboard. It was torn and mended and I tried to reconstruct it. Now I've designed a new variation and let the star wander onto a hat and some socks. When you knit these mittens, give them your full attention. Double check your work when knitting the mirror-image left mitten. If you want larger size mittens, use thicker yarn and needles.

LEVEL OF DIFFICULTY Experienced

YARN 6/2 wool yarn, 328 yds / 300 m per 100 g

YARN AMOUNTS for one pair: color 1 black .7 oz/20 g, color 2 white 1.4 oz/40 g

NEEDLES set of 5 dpn US sizes 0 and 2.5 / 2 and 3 mm; stitch holders

GAUGE 29 sts in pattern on larger ndls = 4 in / 10 cm.
Adjust needle sizes to obtain correct gauge if necessary.

FINISHED MEASUREMENTS width 3 ¾ in / 9.5 cm, length 11 in / 28 cm

With smaller dpn and color 2, CO 48 sts. Divide sts over 4 dpn and join, being careful not to twist cast-on row. Work in k2, p2 ribbing as follows: 1 ¼ in / 3 cm color 2, 2 rnds color 1, 2 rnds color 2, 2 rnds color 1, 1 ¼ in / 3 cm color 2. Change to larger dpn and charted pattern (see next page). Work 2 rnds in stockinette with color 2 and then inc 2 sts on the 2nd rnd with m1 between ndls 2 and 3 and m1 between ndls 1 and 4 until there are 50 sts total.

Work 2 rnds in pattern and then 2 rnds with color 2, following the chart. Make sure that the stranded knitting doesn't pull in.

THUMB GUSSET On the next rnd, begin shaping thumb gusset: K1 with color 2 and k1 with color 1, m1 with color 2, and k3 with color 2, m1 with color 2 and k1 with color 1. Repeat this increase on every other rnd (there will be 2 more sts between increases each time) a total of 5 times. When piece reaches end of thumb gusset (see chart), place 15 sts (= 1 + 13 + 1 sts) onto holder.

On the next rnd, CO 13 sts over thumbhole and continue following chart until 10 sts rem. The top shaping is made with k2tog tbl at beg of ndls 1 and 3 and k2tog at end of ndls 2 and 4. Cut yarn and pull through remaining sts.

THUMB Divide the 15 thumb sts onto dpn and pick up and knit 13 sts along top of thumbhole + 1 st at each side = 30 sts total. Work following the chart until 10 sts remain. Cut yarn and pull through remaining sts.

SECOND MITTEN Work as for first, reversing placement of thumb and motifs.

■ = knit with color 1

□ = knit with color 2

STARS

This style of socks used to be called "pjäx" or ski boot socks. In this version, they've become very fine socks. The doubled cuff makes them warm and the foot knit with a single strand of yarn fits nicely. The heel flap is reinforced and continues into the heel gusset and band for the best fit. Some ribbed stripes are hidden under the cuff as for the Stars hat. The striped toe makes it easy to keep track of the toe decrease rows.

LEVEL OF DIFFICULTY Experienced

YARN 6/2 wool yarn, 328 yds / 300 m per 100 g

YARN AMOUNTS for 1 pair: color 1 black .88 oz/25 g, color 2 white 2.5 oz/80 g

NEEDLES set of 5 dpn US sizes 1.5 and 2.5 / 2.5 and 3 mm

GAUGE 27 sts in pattern on larger ndls or 28 sts in stockinette on smaller ndls = 4 in / 10 cm.

Adjust needle sizes to obtain correct gauge if necessary.

FINISHED MEASUREMENTS leg length 10 ¾ in / 27 cm (when turned down 7 ½ in / 19 cm), foot length: 9 ¾ in / 25 cm; leg width 5 ¼ in / 13 cm

With smaller dpn and color 1, CO 72 sts. Divide sts evenly over 4 dpn and join, being careful not to twist cast-on row. Work in stockinette for 4 rnds. Turn so that the WS faces out – rolled edge. Change to color 2 and knit 1 rnd. Change to 3 larger size dpn (one ndl for each pattern repeat simplifies the knitting). Work in charted pattern. Make sure that the stranding doesn't pull in the knitting! Change to 4 smaller size dpn and knit 1 rnd with color 2 and then knit 1 rnd with color 1. Turn work and knit 7 rnds in stockinette with color 1 = rolled edge. Change to color 2 and purl 1 rnd. Now work in k2, p2 ribbing, decreasing 8 sts evenly spaced around (*k2tog, k7; rep from * around) on the first rnd = 64 sts rem.

Continue in ribbing in the following color sequence: 1 ¼ in / 3 cm color 2, 2 rnds color 1, 2 rnds color 2, 2 rnds color 1, 1 ¾ in / 4.5 cm color 2. Move the sts on the ndls one st to the right to center the ribbing pattern – begin and end round with k1.

HEEL (COMBINED GUSSET AND HEEL BAND) The heel flap is worked back and forth with color 2 over the sts from ndls 1 and 4 so place those sts onto one ndl. Begin on WS and purl 32 across and then work 30 rows in reinforced heel pattern (Eye of Partridge) as follows:

Row 1: Sl 1 purlwise, *k1, sl 1 purlwise wyb*; rep * to * across.

Row 2: Sl 1 purlwise, purl rem sts.

Row 3: Sl 1 purlwise, sl 1 purlwise wyb, k1*; rep * to * across.

Row 4: Purl.

Repeat rows 1-4.

HEEL GUSSET Begin on RS: K20, turn.

Sl 1 purlwise, p7, turn.

Sl 1 purlwise, k8, turn.

Sl 1 purlwise, p9, turn.

Continue the same way, adding 1 more st on every row and end with sl 1st st, p15, turn.

■ = knit with color 1
□ = knit with color 2

HEEL BAND Sl 1 purlwise, k14, k2tog tbl (the 15th st is on top), turn
Sl 1 purlwise, p14, p2tog, turn.
Repeat these 2 rows until 16 sts remain.

Place 8 sts each onto ndls 1 and 4 and pick up and knit 17 sts on each side of heel flap. On the next rnd, knit each of the picked-up sts through back loop. Work in stockinette over sts on ndls 1 and 4 and k2, p2 ribbing over ndls 2 and 3. Dec at the end of ndl 1 and beg of ndl 4 on every 3rd rnd 11 times until 60 sts total remain. Divide the sts evenly over 4 dpn. Work as set until foot is 5 ¼ in / 13 cm from heel flap. The toe will be 2 ½ in / 6.5 cm long.

TOE SHAPING Change to color 1 and work 2-row wide stockinette stripes over all sts, Knit 1 rnd. On the next rnd, k2tog at the end of each ndl and repeat this dec with 5, then 4, 3, 2 rounds, and finally 1 round between decrease rnds and then dec on every rnd until 8 sts rem. Cut yarn and pull through rem sts.

SECOND SOCK Work as for first sock.

BAGGY

After single-color and striped socks, lice-patterned socks are the next easiest. The extra strand of yarn makes the socks warmer and thicker in your shoes. The toes and peasant heels are easy to replace if they wear out. The heels and toes are shaped as for a mitten top. To reinforce them, they are knit with two strands of the same color yarn that are twisted around each other on the inside.

LEVEL OF DIFFICULTY Intermediate

YARN 6/2 wool yarn, 328 yds / 300 m per 100 g

YARN AMOUNTS for 1 pair: color 1 gray 1.4 oz/40 g, color 2 white 1 oz/30 g

NEEDLES set of 5 dpn US sizes 1.5 and 2.5 / 2.5 and 3 mm

GAUGE 27 sts in pattern on larger ndls = 4 in / 10 cm.
Adjust needle sizes to obtain correct gauge if necessary.

FINISHED MEASUREMENTS leg length 9 ¾ in / 25 cm, foot length:
9 ¾ in / 25 cm, leg width 4 ¼ in / 11 cm, foot width 3 ¾ in / 9.5 cm

With smaller dpn and color 1, CO 60 sts. Divide sts evenly over 4 dpn and join, being careful not to twist cast-on row. Work in k2, p2 ribbing for ¾ in / 2 cm. Change to color 2 and work another 1 ¾ in / 2 cm in ribbing (knit the first rnd for a smooth color transition). Change to larger ndls and color 1. Work in charted pattern for 5 ½ in / 14 cm. Make sure that the stranding doesn't pull in the knitting.

With smooth contrast color waste yarn, knit the sts on ndls 2 and 3 (= foot). Knit a complete rnd with color 1.

HEEL (PEASANT HEEL WITH BAND SHAPING) Change to two strands of color 2, alternating the strands for reinforcement: *K1 with one strand, k1 with the other strand*; rep * to * around. Twist the strands around each other on WS in one direction for half the row and in the opposite direction on the other half. Do not pull the strands too tightly! Continue for ¾ in / 2 cm and then begin decreasing. On 1st and 3rd ndls, when 3 sts rem, k2tog. On ndls 2 and 4, at beg of ndl, k1 and then ssk. Dec on every round until 12 sts remain. Cut yarn and pull through rem sts.

FOOT Remove the waste yarn and pick up 62 sts around foot and work the first rnd with the 2 extra sts. Work in

pattern with colors 1 and 2 for 2 rnds. Dec at the end of ndl 1 and beg of ndl 4 on every other rnd 4 times until 52 sts remain. Divide rem sts over 4 dpn.

Work in pattern for 5 ¼ in / 13 cm. The toe will be 2 ¼ in / 5.5 cm long.

Change to color 2 (cut color 1) and work the toe with 2 strands of yarn as for the heel so it will be reinforced. Shape toe as for heel.

SECOND SOCK Work as for first sock.

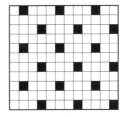

☐ = knit with color 1
■ = knit with color 2

SPRUCE

The spruce-patterned garments in this book were inspired by a small child's cotton stocking found in the Regional Museum in Kristianstad, Sweden. You can design your own spruce pattern by shifting and turning the branches and horizontal panels! The heels and toes are reinforced by knitting them with two alternating strands of yarn. The toes are knitted with two colors for a tweed-like effect.

LEVEL OF DIFFICULTY Intermediate

YARN 6/2 wool yarn, 328 yds / 300 m per 100 g

YARN AMOUNTS for 1 pair: color 1 white 2.5 oz/70 g, color 2 red 1 oz/30 g

NEEDLES set of 6 dpn US sizes 1.5 and 2.5 / 2.5 and 3 mm

GAUGE 27 sts in pattern on larger ndls or 28 sts in stockinette on smaller ndls = 4 in / 10 cm. Adjust needle sizes to obtain correct gauge if necessary.

FINISHED MEASUREMENTS leg length 12 ½ in / 31.5 cm, foot length: 9 ¾ in / 25 cm, leg width 4 ¼ in / 11 cm, foot width 3 ¾ in / 9.5 cm

With smaller dpn and color 1, CO 60 sts. Divide sts evenly over 4 dpn and join, being careful not to twist cast-on row. Work in k2, p2 ribbing for 1 ½ in / 4 cm. Change to larger ndls (divide sts over 5 dpn with 1 repeat on each ndl) and work charted pattern. Make sure that the stranding doesn't pull in the knitting.

Change to smaller ndls when pattern is complete and then work in stockinette with color 1 for ¾ in / 2 cm.

With smooth contrast color waste yarn, knit the sts on ndls 2 and 3 (= foot). Knit a complete rnd with color 1.

HEEL (PEASANT HEEL WITH BAND SHAPING) Change to larger ndls and two strands of color 2, alternating the strands for reinforcement: *K1 with one strand, k1 with the other strand*; rep * to * around. Twist the strands around each other on WS in one direction for half the row and in the opposite direction on the other half. Do not pull the strands too tightly! Continue for ¾ in / 2 cm and then begin decreasing. On 1st and 3rd ndls, when 3 sts rem, k2tog. On ndls 2 and 4, at beg of ndl, k1 and then ssk. Dec on every round until 12 sts remain. Cut yarn and pull through rem sts.

FOOT Remove the waste yarn and, with smaller dpn, pick up 62 sts and work 2 rnds in stockinette with color 1. Dec at the end of ndl 1 and beg of ndl 4 on every other rnd 4 times until 54 sts remain. Divide rem sts over 4 dpn 14-13-14-13. Work until foot is 5 ¼ in / 13 cm from heel. The toe will be 2 ¼ in / 5.5 cm long.

Change to larger ndls and add color 2 and work the 2-color pattern following the chart for ¾ in / 2 cm. Now decrease: Ndls 1 and 3: when 4 sts rem on ndls, k2tog, k2. Ndls 2 and 4, K1, ssk at beg of ndl. Dec on every rnd until 14 sts remain. Cut yarn.

SECOND SOCK Work as for first sock.

☐ = knit with color 1
■ = knit with color 2

RAGG (HEAVY RAGG)

Here are two very basic socks in two thicknesses. The heel flap is reinforced and the heel gusset is easy to knit and fits well.

LEVEL OF DIFFICULTY Intermediate

YARN single (doubled) 6/2 wool yarn, 328 yds / 300 m per 100 g

YARN AMOUNTS for 1 pair: color 1 blue 1.75 oz/50 g (black 2.5 oz/70 g), color 2 gray 1.4 oz/40 g (blue 1.75 oz/50 g)

NEEDLES set of 5 dpn US size 1.5 / 2.5 mm (US 4 / 3.5 mm)

GAUGE 28 (20) sts in stockinette = 4 in / 10 cm. Adjust needle size to obtain correct gauge if necessary.

FINISHED MEASUREMENTS leg length 9 ¾ in / 25 cm, foot length 9 ¾ in / 25 cm

With single (doubled) strand of color 1, CO 64 (48) sts. Divide sts evenly over 4 dpn and join, being careful not to twist cast-on row. Work in k2, p2 ribbing with 12 repeats of 6- (5-) row stripes in colors 1 and 2 (knit 1st rnd of new color for a smooth transition). Catch unused color after every 3rd (2nd) rnd. Move the sts one st to the right on the final rnd to center the ribbing = begin and end rnd with k1.

HEEL (GUSSET HEEL) The heel flap is worked back and forth with color 1 over the sts on ndls 1 and 4. Move those sts to one needle. Begin on WS and purl 32 (24) across and then work 30 (24) rows in reinforced heel stitch (Eye of Partridge) as follows:
Row 1: Sl 1 purlwise, *k1, sl 1 purlwise wyb*; rep * to * across.
Row 2: Sl 1 purlwise, purl rem sts.
Row 3: Sl 1 purlwise, sl 1 purlwise wyb, k1*; rep * to * across.
Row 4: Purl.
Repeat rows 1-4.

HEEL GUSSET K17 (13), k2tog tbl, k1, turn.
Sl 1, p3, p2tog, p1, turn. Sl 1, k4, k2tog tbl, k1, turn.
Sl 1, p5, p2tog, p1, turn.
Continue the same way until all the side sts have been eliminated and 18 (14) sts remain. Divide heel gusset sts over ndls 1 and 4 and pick up and knit 16 (13) sts along each side of heel flap. On the next rnd, knit the picked-up sts through back loops. Beginning with color 1, work in striped stockinette over sts of ndls 1 and 4 and in striped ribbing over ndls 2 and 3. Work 2 rnds. Next, dec at the end of ndl 1 and beg of ndl 4 on every other rnd 11 (10) times until 60 (44) sts rem. Divide the rem sts evenly over 4 dpn. Work until 10 (8) stripes from the heel flap = about 5 ¼ in / 13 cm (4 ¾ in / 12 cm). The toe will be 2 ⅜ in / 6 cm (2 ¾ in / 7 cm) long.

TOE SHAPING Knit 1 rnd in stockinette with color 1. On the next rnd, k2tog at the end of each ndl and repeat this dec with 5, then 4, 3, 2 rounds, and finally 1 round between decrease rnds and then dec on every rnd until 8 sts rem. Cut yarn and pull through rem sts.

SECOND SOCK Work as for first sock.

BLOCKS

Blocks takes some time to knit because the strands must be twisted around each other but the result is a well-made and heavy pair of socks. Read the instructions carefully so you'll understand how to handle the stranding. The socks feature a classic Dutch heel with a heel flap and band underneath. It's automatically reinforced by the way it's knit.

LEVEL OF DIFFICULTY Experienced

YARN 6/2 wool yarn, 328 yds / 300 m per 100 g

YARN AMOUNTS for 1 pair: color 1 black 1.75 oz/50 g, color 2 red 1.75 oz/50 g

NEEDLES straight ndls US size 1.5 / 2.5 mm and set of 5 dpn US sizes 2.5 and 4 / 3 and 3.5 mm

GAUGE 27 sts in pattern on largest dpn = 4 in / 10 cm.
Adjust needle sizes to obtain correct gauge if necessary.

FINISHED MEASUREMENTS leg length 10 ¼ in / 26 cm, foot length: 9 ½ in / 24 cm, leg width 4 ¼ in / 11 cm, foot width 3 ¾ in / 9.5 cm

With straight ndls and color 1, CO 60 sts and work back and forth in garter stitch. Knit 1 row with color 1, 2 rows with color 2, and 2 rows with color 1. Change to dpn US 2.5 / 3 mm; divide sts evenly over 4 ndls and join. Work in stripe pattern for 1 ½ in / 4 cm following the chart. Twist the strands around each other on the back, twisting in one direction for the first half of the rnd and in the opposite direction on the other half. Do not pull the strands too tightly!

Change to dpn US 4 / 3.5 mm and block pattern (see chart) for 5 ¼ in / 13 cm. Move one st from the 3rd to the 4th dpn to center the pattern.

HEEL (DUTCH HEEL) Work the heel flap back and forth with ndls US 2.5 / 3 mm and the stitches from ndls 1 and 4 (place these 31 sts all on one ndl). Work in stripe pattern, with color 1 as the edge sts for 20 rows = 2 ¼ in / 5.5 cm. Always slip the first st of every row (= edge st).

HEEL BAND Continue on US 2.5 / 3 mm ndls and stripe pattern. With RS facing, k22 including the slipped edge st, k2tog tbl (with color 1 over the other st), turn.
Sl 1, p13, p2tog, turn.
Sl 1, k13, k2tog tbl, turn.
Sl 1, p13, p2tog, turn. Continue the same way until 15 sts rem. Change to US 4 / 3.5 mm dpn. Place 8 sts onto ndl 1

and 7 sts onto ndl 4 and pick up and knit 17 sts along each side of heel flap. Knit the picked-up sts through back loop on the first rnd.
Begin with stripe pattern on ndl 1 and then switch to block pattern starting on ndl 2. Continuing in blocks around, knit 2 rnds.

GUSSET When 3 sts rem on ndl 1, k2tog with color 1, k1; on ndl 4, k1 and then k2tog tbl (with color 1 on top of other color). Dec the same way on every other rnd until 54 sts rem.
Divide the sts 14-13-14-13 over 4 dpn. Work in block pattern until foot measures 5 ¼ in / 13 cm from heel flap. The toe will be 2 ½ in / 6.5 cm long.

TOE SHAPING Change to US 2.5 / 3 mm dpn and knit 1 rnd in stripe pattern. On the next rnd, k2tog at the end of each ndl and repeat the dec rnd with 5 rnds, then 3 rnds, and finally 1 rnd between decrease rnds and then on every rnd until 10 sts rem. Cut yarn and pull through rem sts. Seam the garter stitch at top of leg.

SECOND SOCK Work as for first sock.

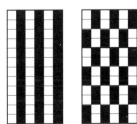

■ = knit with color 1
□ = knit with color 2

TWEED

Two strands of yarn are held together to make these socks strong and good for wearing on cold floors and with heavy boots. The heel and toe are knitted the same way. The toe is joi-ned to the top of the foot with three-needle bind-off. This sock is construc-ted as for machine-knit socks.

LEVEL OF DIFFICULTY Intermediate

YARN doubled 6/2 wool yarn, 328 yds / 300 m per 100 g

YARN AMOUNTS for 1 pair: color 1 pink 2.5 oz/70 g, color 2 red 2.5 oz/70 g

NEEDLES set of 5 dpn US size 4 / 3.5 mm

GAUGE 20 sts in stockinette = 4 in / 10 cm.
Adjust needle size to obtain correct gauge if necessary.

FINISHED MEASUREMENTS leg length 9 ¾ in / 25 cm, foot length: 9 ¾ in / 25 cm

With 2 strands of color 1 held together, CO 48 sts. Divide sts over 4 dpn (12 sts each) and join, being careful not to twist cast-on row. Work in k1, p1 ribbing for 1 ½ in / 4 cm. Cut 1 strand of color 1 and add a strand of color 2 (= 1 strand of each color held together) and work in k3, p1 ribbing until sock leg measures 7 ½ in / 19 cm. Now work heel with 2 strands of color 2.

SHORT ROW HEEL Ndl 1: knit until 1 st rem; turn. Sl 1 purlwise, purl rem sts.
Ndl 4: purl to until 1 st rem; turn. Sl 1 and knit rem sts across.
Note: Tighten yarn slightly when turning to avoid a hole.
Continue the same way, turning 1 st earlier than for previous turn on every row.
Last row: Ndl 4: p3; turn.

With one strand of each color held together, work 1 rnd over sts on all 4 ndls, with k3, p1 ribbing over ndls 2 and 3. On this round, m1 (lift strand between sts and knit into back loop) on each side between ndls 1 and 2 and between ndls 3 and 4.

Change to two strands of color 2.
Ndl 1: K4; turn. Slip 1 and then purl across.
Ndl 4: P4; turn, sl 1 and then knit across.
Continue the same way, with 1 st more for each row until all the sts have been worked. Change to 1 strand of each color and, on the first rnd, knit the 2 extra sts tog so 48 sts remain.
Continue in stockinette on the sts of ndls 1 and 4, and k3, p1 ribbing on ndls 2 and 3, except for the last purl on ndl 3 which is knit instead.
Make a dec at the end of ndl 1 and beg of ndl 4 every 6th rnd 4 times until 40 sts rem.
Divide the sts evenly over the dpn. Continue ribbing and stockinette as set and work until foot measures 4 ¼ in / 11 cm from heel. The toe will be 2 ¾ in / 7 cm long.

TOE SHAPING Change to two strands of color 2 and work in stockinette for ¾ in / 2 cm. Work toe as for short row heel but only with color 2 and knit sts. Do not pick up 2 extra sts. End with the last purl row on ndl 4.
Turn knitting inside out and work from the WS. Using a single strand of color 1, join 1 st from ndl 3 with 1 st of ndl 4 and bind off at the same time (= three-needle bind-off). Work the same way with the sts on ndls 2 and 1.

SECOND SOCK Work as for first sock.

SPIRAL (HEAVY SPIRAL)

If you don't like to knit heels, then these are the socks for you! By shifting the ribbing, the sock forms around your foot and wears evenly.

LEVEL OF DIFFICULTY Easy

YARN single (doubled) 6/2 wool yarn, 328 yds / 300 m per 100 g

YARN AMOUNTS for one pair: color 1 yellow green 2 oz/60 g (red 3.5 oz/100 g), color 2 red .7 oz/20 g (gray 1.4 oz/40 g)

NEEDLES set of 5 dpn US size 1.5 (6) / 2.5 (4) mm

GAUGE 28 (19) sts in stockinette = 4 in / 10 cm

FINISHED MEASUREMENTS length 15 (17) in / 38 (43) cm

With one (two) strands of color 2 yarn, CO 60 (48) sts. Divide sts evenly over 4 dpn and join, being careful not to twist cast-on row. Work in k1, p1 ribbing for 1 ½ in / 4 cm. Change to color 1 and knit 1 rnd and then work in k3, p3 ribbing. On the 5th rnd, move the sts 1 st to the left. Shift sts the same way on every 5th rnd 24 (18) times = about 11 ¾ (13) in / 30 (33) cm.

TOE SHAPING Change to color 2 and stockinette. Alternate colors 2 and 1 for 3-row wide stripes on toe. Knit 1 rnd.
K4, k2tog; rep * to * around.
Knit 5 rnds.
K3, k2tog; rep * to * around.
Knit 4 rnds.
K2, k2tog; rep * to * around.
Knit 3 rnds.
K1, k2tog; rep * to * around.
Knit 2 rnds.
K2tog around. Cut yarn and pull tail through rem sts.

SECOND SOCK Make as for first sock.

ANKLE WARMERS

What do you do when your feet are cold and your shoes are too tight for wool socks? Of course, you knit some ankle warmers! Quick, cozy, and warm. I've used the sock leg patterns from this book and the knitting technique from a hat. The possibilities are endless. Notice how the band under the foot is knit so the widest part is in front.

Tweed

LEVEL OF DIFFICULTY Easy
YARN DOUBLED 6/2 wool yarn, 328 yds / 300 m per 100 g
YARN AMOUNTS for one pair: color 1 light blue 1.4 oz/40 g, color 2 blue 1.4 oz/40 g
NEEDLES set of 5 dpn US size 4 / 3.5 mm
FINISHED MEASUREMENTS length at center back 6 ¾ in / 17 cm

With two strands of color 1 held together, CO 48 sts. Divide sts over 4 dpn and join, being careful not to twist cast-on row.

Work in k1, p1 ribbing for 1 ½ in / 4 cm. Change to one strand each of colors 1 and 2 and work in k3, p1 ribbing until piece is 7 ½ in / 19 cm long. With smooth contrast color waste yarn, knit the sts on ndls 2 and 3 (foot opening). Cut color 1 and add a second strand of color 2. Knit 1 rnd. Work in k1, p1 ribbing for 5 rnds and then BO loosely (= heel opening). Remove waste yarn and pick up 52 sts. Knit 1 rnd with color 2 and then work in k1, p1 ribbing for 4 rnds. Dec 1 st at end of ndl 1 and dec 1 st at beginning of ndl 4 on every other rnd 3 times until 46 sts remain. Work 1 rnd in ribbing and then BO loosely.

SECOND ANKLE WARMER Work as for first.

Heavy Ragg

LEVEL OF DIFFICULTY Easy
YARN doubled 6/2 wool yarn, 328 yds / 300 m per 100 g
YARN AMOUNTS for one pair: color 1 red 1.75 oz/50 g, color 2 yellow-green .7 oz/20 g
NEEDLES set of 5 dpn US size 4 / 3.5 mm
FINISHED MEASUREMENTS length at center back 6 ¼ in / 16 cm

With two strands of color 1 held together, CO 48 sts. Divide sts over 4 dpn and join, being careful not to twist cast-on row.

Work in k2, p2 ribbing for 9 five-row wide stripes alternating colors 1 and 2. Catch unused color on every other rnd.

With smooth contrast color waste yarn, knit the sts on ndls 2 and 3 (foot opening). Continue in ribbing with color 1 for 5 rnds and then BO loosely (= heel opening). Remove waste yarn and pick up 52 sts. Work in ribbing with color 1 for 4 rnds. Dec 1 st at end of ndl 1 and dec 1 st at beginning of ndl 4 on every other rnd 3 times until 46 sts remain. Work 1 rnd in ribbing and then BO loosely.

SECOND ANKLE WARMER Work as for first.

Heavy Bonnet

LEVEL OF DIFFICULTY Easy
YARN doubled 6/2 wool yarn, 328 yds / 300 m per 100 g
YARN AMOUNTS for one pair: color 1 black 1.75 oz/50 g, color 2 gray .7 oz/20 g
NEEDLES straight ndls and set of 5 dpn US size 6 / 4 mm
FINISHED MEASUREMENTS length at center back 6 ¾ in / 17 cm

With straight ndls and two strands of color 1 held together, CO 48 sts. Work back and forth in garter st. Knit 1 row (= WS). Now work in stripe pattern: color 1 2 rows, *color 2 4 rows, color 1 4 rows*; rep * to * until there are a total of 13 stripes. Catch unused strand at side on every other row.

Knit 1 row with color 1 and then divide sts over 4 dpn and join. Work 4 rnds in stockinette with color 1.

With smooth contrast color waste yarn, knit the sts on ndls 2 and 3 (foot opening). Knit 1 rnd with color 1 and then work in k2, p2 ribbing for 5 rnds. BO loosely (= heel opening). Remove waste yarn and pick up 52 sts. Work in k2, p2 ribbing with color 1 for 4 rnds. Dec 1 st at end of ndl 1 and dec 1 st at beginning of ndl 4 on every other rnd 3 times until 46 sts remain. Work 1 rnd in ribbing and then BO loosely.

FINISHING With RS facing, join back of leg with mattress stitch.

SECOND ANKLE WARMER Work as for first.

SPRUCE ANKLE WARMERS

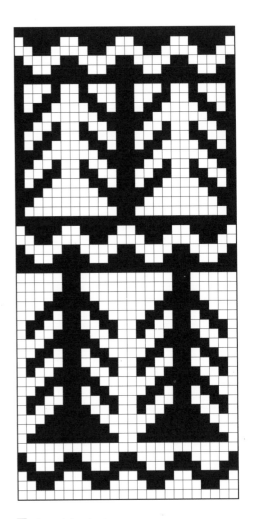

☐ = knit with color 1
■ = knit with color 2

LEVEL OF DIFFICULTY Intermediate

YARN 6/2 wool yarn, 328 yds / 300 m per 100 g

YARN AMOUNTS for one pair: color 1 blue 1 oz/30 g, color 2 white .7 oz/20 g

NEEDLES straight ndls US size 1.5 / 2.5 mm; set of 6 dpn US sizes 1.5 and 2.5 / 2.5 and 3 mm

FINISHED MEASUREMENTS length at center back 7 in / 18 cm

With color 1 and straight needles, CO 60 sts and work back and forth in garter stitch for 5 rows.

Change to larger dpn, dividing sts over 5 dpn (one for each pattern repeat makes the knitting easier). Join, and knit 1 rnd. Now work in charted pattern. Make sure that the stranding doesn't pull in the knitting.

After completing charted rows, change to smaller dpn and color 1 and work in stockinette for 6 rnds. With smooth contrast color waste yarn, knit the stitches on ndls 2 and 3 (= foot opening). Knit 1 rnd with color 1.

Now work in k2, p2 ribbing for ¾ in / 2 cm. BO loosely (= heel opening).

Remove the waste yarn and pick up 64 sts. Work in ribbing with color 1 for 6 rnds. Dec 1 st at end of ndl 1 and dec 1 st at beginning of ndl 4 on every other rnd 4 times until 56 sts remain. Work another 2 rnds in ribbing and then BO loosely.

SECOND ANKLE WARMER Work as for first.

WOOL – A FANTASTIC NATURAL MATERIAL

BY KERSTIN PARADIS GUSTAFSSON

Wool is a natural material that exhibits many wonderful qualities either by itself or when blended with other fibers. There are many different types of wool so you can find the right one for anything from fine soft baby clothes, underwear, and fine suiting to heavy work garments and sportswear as well as all sorts of furnishing textiles and tapestry weavings.

The good qualities of wool

Wool insulates against both heat and cold. It doesn't transfer heat out; instead, thanks to its crimp structure, wool holds in body heat. It has a high elasticity, particularly when damp. That means that wool clothing can be hung out for smoothing when it is wrinkled. Wool resists water and doesn't become wet easily. Wool also holds water well without feeling wet and can hold twice as much as cotton. For that reason, wool clothing is comfortable for wearing directly on the body. Wool is the only fiber that felts when agitated. These are all very good qualities for those of us in the northern part of the globe. By wearing wool garments or even living in felted wool yurts, we are protected against rain, snow, and cold winds. Wool clothes are supple and easy to iron under a damp pressing cloth. When correctly pressed, the fabric retains the shaping or deliberate creasing. If you wear the garment and stretch it, it will regain its original shape when it relaxes.

Certain types of wool, particularly those of the Nordic sheep races, are very lustrous and make beautiful art weaving yarns. Wool fiber isn't very strong as is but it gains strength from other wool qualities, such as high elasticity. The yarn's strength can easily be enhanced depending on, for example, how it is prepared and how much twist is added when spun. Wool is flame retardant and won't burn, but will begin to carbonize at temperatures over about 266° F / 130° Celsius. For that reason, firemen always wear wool clothes. Wool absorbs dye easily and takes up all the dye matter from the water.

WASHING AND HANDLING Airing out woolen garments in damp air is better than washing for everyday care. Clothes worn next to the body probably need to be washed occasionally but outer clothing and rugs usually only need airing out and brushing. Wool doesn't tolerate alkaline materials very well and certainly not high temperatures. Be careful to rinse soap out completely after washing. Wool tolerates acids better so you can use a little white vinegar in the last rinse water. Wool is sensitive to temperature shocks so be careful when washing so the wool doesn't lose its luster, softness and elasticity. Wash at a maximum of 104°F / 40°C but preferably cooler. The lower the temperature, the more time wool, yarn, or garments can soak in the wash water. Don't wash woolens with regular washing detergent. Dish soap or hair shampoo (those without dyes or perfume are best) or safe wool washes formulated for lower temperatures are the best choices for washing wool.

Wool products can be damaged by harmful insects such as beetles or some moth species. For that reason, use wool products often so that they don't lie buried in the dresser drawer where destructive insects can find them and make themselves at home. Wool textiles should be aired out and brushed every now and again. Remove any stains as soon as possible.

Wool is Hair

All mammals have some sort of hair on their bodies. The hair can be thick and long or fine and short. It is called wool when it is soft and fine and hair when it is coarse. Wool has different looks and characteristics depending on what animal it comes from. In Sweden there are several breeds of sheep. All these breeds have various types of wool with correspondingly different qualities. There are also animals whose wool is used by man. The most common wool producing animals besides sheep are goats, camels, and llamas.

WOOL FIBERS There are three types of wool fibers: outer coat hair, undercoat wool, and kemp. All these types can be found in more or less pronounced form on the various sheep breeds. There are many breeds of sheep, each with its own distinct type and quality of wool fiber You can find a suitable wool for almost any project but not every wool will work for each and every end product. All wool fibers are covered with a layer of scales, the epidermal scales or cuticle. The appearance of these scales differs depending on the wool type. They extend from the root to the top as scales on a fish. Outer coat hair is long, coarse, strong, and wavy. Cuticle scales on the coarse fibers usually adjoin each other from edge to edge, which makes water shed quite well. Undercoat wool is fine, short, and finely crimped hair. Here the scales overlap each other like shingles but they can also go around the whole fiber. Kemp is more or less hollow or medulated, thick and easily broken; it doesn't absorb dye well. Now only primitive sheep usually have kemp because it has been selected out from other breeds.

SHEEP BREEDS AND THEIR WOOL Landrace sheep in Sweden and Scandinavia belong to the large group of Northern short-tailed sheep. They have short tails and do not have wool on their legs or faces. Since the early twentieth century, Sweden has had three basic types: Rya sheep, Gotland

Pälsfår (Gotland or "fur" sheep) wool (at left). This wool is about 4 ¾ -5 ¼ in / 12-13 cm long when stretched out. In this sample, you can clearly see where the undercoat ends. The outer (hair) coat has a distinct wave.

Finullsfår (Finnsheep) wool (at right). The length of this wool depends entirely on how often the sheep is shorn. This sample is a full year's growth and it is 2 3/8-2 ¾ in / 6-7 cm long. All the fibers are the same length and have an even crimp.

Rya type wool lock (at right). This wool lock has both undercoat wool and outer coat hair. The undercoat wool makes the lock wide at the base (cut end) and is 2-2 ¾ in / 5-7 cm long in this sample. The outer coat is relatively straight and about 6 ¾ in / 17 cm long.

sheep (also called päls or fur sheep), and Finnsheep plus a few lesser breeds. Their wool is a good example of the different wool types. All are descended from our oldest sheep that were the same type as Gutefår (Gotland Outdoor sheep).

Rya sheep have long and lustrous wool, consisting of a long, coarse wavy outer coat and clearly shorter, finer, and softer undercoat wool. This wool is excellent for socks, outerwear, rugs, and tapestry weavings because it is strong and lustrous.

Gotland wool is very typical with its black skin and legs, and gray wool. There is not much difference between the outer and under coats and the wool is evenly crimped from the root to the tip. It works well for sweaters and woven fabrics for a range of clothing – it's a fine medium quality.

Finnsheep have only fine-fibered wool – they don't have an outer coat. Finnsheep wool is excellent for undergarments and clothing for small children. Because the fibers are so fine, the yarn won't be very durable but, on the other hand, it is very soft.

Gute sheep are the oldest sheep breed and have all types of wool fibers, including kemp. This means that the wool can be prickly depending on how well it was sorted. It is good for outerwear.

The characteristics of wool can vary greatly, so, you must take that into consideration when choosing the type of wool for a particular yarn. These days industry makes that choice for us. If you want to spin your own yarns, you must learn to recognize and understand the qualities of the various wool types. Quality depends in large part on which breed of sheep the wool comes from. Other factors to consider are: is it from a lamb, ewe or ram; was shorn in the spring or the fall; and what part of the body did it come from? The best wool is on the sides of the animal. That is the cleanest and most typical wool for the breed. Lambs have the softest wool and, usually, the older the sheep, the coarser its wool. Ewes between two and five years of age have the best wool and old ewes have the coarsest.

Wool Preparation for Various End Products

The characteristics of a garment or, for example, a rug, don't depend just on the qualities of the wool. The softness, durability, and other characteristics can be enhanced by handling the wool in the right way while processing it through to the finished item. Wool can be carded so that the fibers do not drift apart. Then they can be spun in such a way that the desired qualities are effectively brought out. The yarn for soft children's wear shouldn't be spun and plied too tightly. Yarn for a pair of sports socks should, however, be spun and plied more tightly so that the fibers are properly integrated in the yarn. The next step is weaving or knitting – choose the appropriate technique to match the yarn and end product. An outer garment should be tight, a blanket soft and lofty.

It is very important that, early on in the process, you are clear about the qualities needed for your desired product. Even before you choose the wool, take some time to think through what sort of wool, spinning method, etc, would be best for what you would like to make. Don't forget that, as with all handcraft, your own work and time are the most expensive investments you'll make. The cost of materials is normally lower. So, always choose the best possible wool for felting and spinning, or buy yarn from a respected woolen mill for knitting and weaving.

For a complete list of knitting books, contact:

Trafalgar Square Books
Box 257, Howe Hill Road
North Pomfret, Vermont 05053
800.423.4525
www.trafalgarbooks.com